M000249492

The

HOT TUB
MANIFESTO

The

HOT TUB
MANIFESTO

·················

THE *ENTREPRENEUR'S GUIDE* TO HAVING IT ALL

How We *Positioned, Pivoted,* and *Grew Our Company* to **Support the Lifestyle We Wanted**

CHERYL & LOUIS BIRON
WITH CARL GOULD

HIGHPOINT
EXECUTIVE
PUBLISHING
Extend your strategic reach

WWW.HIGHPOINTPUBS.COM

Copyright © 2017 by Cheryl Biron and Louis Biron

All rights reserved. Published in the United States of America. No part of this book may be reproduced or transmitted in any form or by any means, graphic, electronic or mechanical, including photocopying, recording, taping or by any information storage or retrieval system, without permission in writing from the publisher.

This edition published by Highpoint Executive Publishing.
For information, write to info@highpointpubs.com.

First Edition

ISBN: 978-0-9974157-9-7

Library of Congress Cataloging-in-Publication Data

Biron, Cheryl; Biron, Louis
Hot Tub Manifesto: The Entrepreneur's Guide to Having It All

Summary: "*The Hot Tub Manifesto* presents a personal and compelling entrepreneurs' perspective on how the authors positioned, pivoted, grew, and scaled their company, gaining the freedom and flexibility to support the lifestyle they wanted." – Provided by publisher.

ISBN: 978-0-9974157-9-7 (hardcover)
Business, Entrepreneurship

Library of Congress Control Number: 2017936852

Cover and interior design by Kendra Cagle

Manufactured in the United States of America
10 9 8 7 6 5 4 3 2 1

DEDICATION

· · · · · · · · · · · · · · · · · · ·

To our parents, Amy Bryant, John Yancey, and Lise and Andre Biron, for their support in achieving the life of our dreams, and to our teenage children Alexander and Genevieve for being the wonderfully inspiring lights in our lives.

TABLE OF CONTENTS

· · · · · · · · · · · · · · · ·

FOREWORD
by Verne Harnish

. . . .

Running a business is ultimately about freedom. Cheryl and Louis Biron have become experts in that, as you will see in the pages that follow.

I first met Cheryl and Louis, co-founders of One Horn Transportation and both active Entrepreneurs' Organization (EO) members, back in 2013, during the inaugural Key Executive Program at MIT (Birthing of Giants/Executive Management Program (EMP) for EO members and their leadership teams). This event occurred between the publication of my two books, *Mastering the Rockefeller Habits,* and *Scaling Up, Rockefeller Habits 2.0,* and I was teaching many segments of the four-day course. When we had our private session to discuss their business, I recognized that the Birons had created an interesting, scalable model requiring very few employees by leveraging technology and outsourcing.

Scalability is key to creating freedom through your business. As founder of both EO and Gazelles, my team and I have spent over three decades advising tens of thousands of CEOs and executives to help them navigate the complexities of scaling their business ventures. By the time we met, Cheryl and Louis had scaled One Horn to the point that they were no longer needed 100-percent in the business on a day-to-day basis. And, they achieved all of this while also molding their business around their lifestyle.

That's what this book is about. In *The Hot Tub Manifesto*, Cheryl and Louis share their story about how they achieved their own vision of freedom – the ability to spend more time with their family while working whenever and wherever they want as their business continues to thrive. This is their Simon Sinek "Why" for creating One Horn. Cheryl has also achieved the freedom to build her business coaching practice using the tools I have developed with my team at Gazelles. Having kept in touch with Cheryl on and off over the years, I was delighted when she joined the fold, helping her clients achieve freedom, however they define it.

The Birons have a compelling story as a couple who left corporate America to grow and pivot an entrepreneurial venture together. As you read about their early days, and then take a deeper dive into some of the best practices they developed as they pivoted and scaled One Horn, you will find some very valuable takeaways. In the book's final section, Cheryl and Louis share their personal story of a couple working together, Cheryl's views as a woman in a traditionally male industry, and even an interview with their children on how the Birons' successful business journey has impacted and inspired them.

Indeed, it's all here. In *The Hot Tub Manifesto*, you will find many valuable and practical ideas of how to build, run, and scale your business, giving you an informed and actionable head start toward your own freedom.

Verne Harnish

CEO of Gazelles, Founder of the Entrepreneurs' Organization (EO), and author of *Scaling Up (Rockefeller Habits 2.0)*

ACKNOWLEDGEMENTS

· · · · · · · · · · · · · · · · · ·

First, we want to thank each other for being such wonderful partners in work and in life. We are thrilled to share our story in the hopes that we inspire others to achieve what they consider freedom.

Thank you to Carl Gould, for helping us frame our book to provide the takeaways that would benefit other entrepreneurs and business leaders. We want to pay it forward, since we have benefitted greatly from the experience of others who have shared their stories and specific ideas that have helped us.

We also want to gratefully acknowledge Amy Bryant, Cheryl's mother, who is also an author, for helping proofread our book; Linda Terjesen, who has been one of those advisor friends, strategizing in our hot tub from the beginning, and providing moral support when times were tough; Adele DiBari, another advisor/friend who helped us during some of those hot tub discussions at key pivot points; Cheryl's Wharton Entrepreneur Circle friends and colleagues, including Neil Burns, Howard Kastner, John Sudol, Patricia Preztunik, and Heng Wong, for being a sounding board during the early One Horn years, through all those pivots and reinventions; Solange Perret, for inspiring us to make our biggest change to the agent-based business model; and Tom Patania, an EO friend who helped us coin the term "Think Tank" for our famous Hot Tub, and for his support and encouragement as Cheryl builds her coaching practice.

Finally, thanks to all of the people who met with Cheryl and encouraged her during the soul-searching journey that led to her LexaGen Freedom Accelerator Gazelles coaching practice: Susan Michel, Beth Storz, Mike Goldman, Chandra Gould, Mike Michalowicz, Sally Glick, Pat Roque, and Andy Bailey. And our children, Alexander and Genevieve, who always say to us, "You can do it!" It's great having you in our corner.

A NOTE FROM CHERYL AND LOUIS

· · · · · · · · · · · · · · · · · ·

A few decades ago, the idea of running a family business evoked images of a father-and-son hardware store or a restaurant with Mom running the kitchen and Dad at the cash register. Today, family entrepreneurship is more likely to imply a laptop on the dining room table or a conference call on the way to soccer practice. For us, running a family business often involves taking calls on a customized headset that fits inside a ski helmet or having strategy meetings in our backyard hot tub.

Global connectivity and other revolutionary technological innovations have unleashed an era of unprecedented business freedom for those who know how to take advantage of it. Of course, we had no idea these kinds of options would be available to us when we got married. Both of us graduated from prestigious schools and were at the start of demanding careers (Cheryl in finance and later marketing, Louis in engineering). Our parents encouraged us to follow the path that had worked for their generation: get hired by a big company and work your way up the ladder. If we played our cards right, we were told, we would "succeed" and retire comfortably.

But then downsizing, rightsizing and automation (among other things) turned the corporate world into a cutthroat competition where you had to claw your way to the top or be out of a job. Put in as many hours as your company demanded, or they would find someone else who would. So like many Gen Xer's, we quickly found ourselves stuck on a treadmill of working long days, late nights and way too many weekends.

Soon we added two children into the mix, but most days it felt like we only got to see them when we were rushing to feed them breakfast in the morning or tucking them in at night. What's more, we hardly ever saw each other. It was easy to see how twenty or thirty years could just fly by this way, and we began to wonder: was this really what success was about? Were we supposed to condense all our real living into three weeks of vacation each year until we retired?

In 2005, we decided to get off the treadmill and begin our entrepreneurial adventure. Today that could mean anything from buying a franchise to selling specialty items over the internet. In our case—after some research and many trips to the bank—we found ourselves the proud owners of an office, six tractors, eighty trailers, and a yard in which to store them. We also became responsible for the paychecks of five employees. Just like that, we were in the trucking business.

The immediate result of this move was that we saw a lot more of our children, who were then just four and seven years old. This alone was worth the sacrifice and risk involved in our new endeavor. Still, the adjustment was far from smooth. Our MBAs had not prepared us for customers who didn't pay when they said they would, or for drivers who needed a cash advance before they could complete a delivery.

During those early years, we learned that working in our own business could be just as stressful as working for a demanding boss. Sure, we were spending more time together, and we were having strategy meetings in the hot tub instead of in a stuffy conference room downtown. Still, we hadn't obtained the level of autonomy we wanted. The question was: how could we transform our business so we could have the flexibility and freedom we craved *before* we retired?

As with many issues before, we pondered this question in our hot tub one evening with some of our good friends who also serve as business advisors. And when we emerged from the water that night, we entered the second phase of our entrepreneurial journey. Soon, we had restructured our business in a way that not only reduced our workload and stress, but also greatly increased our growth potential without requiring more capital investment. Instead of molding our lives around our careers—as so many before us had done—we molded our business to fit the lives we wanted as individuals, as a couple, and as a family.

In the pages that follow, we'll explain exactly how we did it. In Part One, "Beginnings and Growth," you'll hear our story— warts and all—and you'll get to laugh at (and learn from!) all our initial missteps and miscalculations. But you'll also see how we were ultimately able to take control of both our business and our personal lives without sacrificing our long term financial wellbeing.

In Part Two, "Building Best Practices," we'll share the technical details of how we run our business while maintaining our desired work-life balance. This includes all our practical advice for scaling up and automating in order to maximize both productivity and growth potential. In Part Three, "Life Lessons," we'll offer our thoughts on broader issues like family priorities and succession planning, along with pragmatic suggestions for working side by side with the person who is your partner both in business and in life.

We all have different ideas about the ideal work week, as well as whether we prefer to spend our extra time on the ski slopes, at the beach, or on a hike. Ultimately, the *Hot Tub Manifesto* is not the only guide for how to run a business. But it is a great way for entrepreneurs to gain both the freedom and the flexibility to live whatever life they choose.

PART ONE
BEGINNINGS AND GROWTH

CHAPTER 1

· · · · · · · · · · · · · · · · · · ·

CORPORATE EXECS

Success can mean very different things to different people, but most of us agree on the basic ingredients. A successful life will involve feelings of satisfaction and fulfillment and time spent with the people we love, *doing* what we love. Money isn't everything, but nonetheless is something we all need; so, part of success is having enough of it. For those of us who don't inherit a large fortune, that almost always requires getting a job or running a business.

Ultimately, most decisions in life involve some sort of trade off. Whether you're choosing a car, a spouse, or a profession, your selection will have advantages and disadvantages. The same is true of working for a company or running your own business: there are pros and cons to each. The key is figuring out which option offers you the best deal, based on your unique preferences and priorities.

Living and Leaving the Corporate Career

This book focuses on all the wonderful benefits that come with being an entrepreneur and how to maximize them. However, Louis and I have extensive experience in both worlds, so we wanted to begin our story with an honest discussion of the positive and negative aspects of working in a corporate job.

Both Louis and I started out in corporate America on very desirable paths. After graduating from Cornell, I began my career as a financial analyst with a large investment banking firm in New York City. My education had prepared me well for the requirements of my job: I knew how to respond to Requests for Proposals (RFPs) from municipalities seeking to finance large projects, and how to structure the financing required for the deal. These were skilled activities that paid well. In addition to a good salary and annual bonus, the company paid for my meals, as well as for a car service to whisk me up the FDR Drive to my Upper East Side apartment each night. Not bad for a kid fresh out of undergraduate school!

However I soon decided that this was not what I wanted to be doing for the next forty years. Often we are taught to look at which jobs will give us the best financial reward for our time, which is certainly an important consideration. Prestige can figure into the equation, too. Back then, plenty of us dreamed of being Tom Wolfe's *Bonfire of the Vanities* character Sherman McCoy, Master of the Universe, living in a Park Avenue co-op and working on Wall Street. However, financial rewards and stature always need to be balanced against how much you enjoy the activity you are being paid to do. Catered meals were nice, but eating lunch and dinner at the office started to get old. The glamour of the car service wore off, too.

Triple-A Method: Analyze, Assess, Act!

Back then, as a 23-year-old, I didn't realize I had a system, but in hindsight, it is how I made every pivot in my career and business. While writing my business school applications, I analyzed what I liked and didn't like about my investment banking job and environment. Then I assessed alternative majors and actually created the position of brand manager in my head. While attending a career fair, I discovered it was an actual "thing". A brand manager is a marketing role where I could work on a more tangible product and have a "big picture" view of an entire business—the brand—with the support of the corporate resources to build that business. In hindsight, it is also very entrepreneurial, foreshadowing my future as an entrepreneur. So I acted, changing professions, while I earned my MBA. (In future chapters, we will make mention of our "Triple-A Method" as we made changes in our life.)

I chose the Wharton School of the University of Pennsylvania to earn my MBA in Marketing and Multinational Management, so I could also pursue my interest in working in France. Having been an avid Francophile since high school, the only way to fully master the language was to actually live in a French-speaking environment. After graduation, I began to work for a large consumer packaged goods company in brand management and spent two amazing years in Paris, where I had met Louis on exchange during business school.

Those early-career jobs offered many advantages. When you work for a large company, there are many vital components of the business that you simply do not have to worry about. You never think about the rent or the mortgage on the building where you work or paying the utility bills to keep the lights on and the water running. You are supplied with an office, a computer and even an assistant. The cleaning staff keeps the building tidy, and the accounting department makes sure the bills get paid.

You might deal with a budget for your specific department, and you may sometimes be pressured to accomplish more with less money. But you ultimately don't have to worry about where the money for that budget will come from. If a customer doesn't pay a bill, that's not really your problem.

An established company will also have all its internal systems already set up. As an employee, you are responsible for carrying out the tasks in your job description. In MBA positions, you must also go above and beyond your basic responsibilities in order to get ahead. As a brand manager, I dealt with sales, advertising, operations, product development and accounting, but I had the support of a huge corporation behind all those activities.

Even high ranking executives who are expected to think strategically for the company as a whole are able to delegate a lot of the day-to-day details to others. You may have to develop a comprehensive marketing strategy for the rollout of a new product, but you still don't have to file the company's tax returns, pick up carpet and paint samples for the new office renovation, or make sure the invoices are sent out on time.

And then of course there's the paycheck. Every two weeks, a predictable amount of money appears in your bank account, which you can count on along with ongoing benefits, like health and dental insurance, a retirement account, and maybe even stock options. You might get a company car and a company credit card for expenses, and all kinds of other perks at your disposal. This kind of financial stability and security is nothing to take lightly.

But even with all those very real advantages, corporate life simply wasn't for me. When Louis and I returned to the United States from Paris, my career continued to advance. I got promoted, changing companies when I was offered a position with a higher salary and more responsibility. I continued in my role as a marketing specialist managing various product lines, branching out into everything from pharmaceuticals to health and beauty products. My career was going exactly the way I thought I wanted it to go, but my life was not.

Ultimately, I realized that I was no longer willing to make the sacrifices that my job demanded from me. My priorities had changed. I had a husband and two young children, and I wanted to share more of my life with them. I didn't want to miss my kids' childhood, and I didn't want to wait until retirement to do the things I enjoyed.

The time I was expected to be in the office was compounded by a commute that was over an hour each way. Unfortunately, like many other families, it seemed like the only way we could have a backyard for the kids in a desirable school district was to spend ten or more hours a week fighting traffic. This meant Louis and I were up and out of the house early, and had to rely on a string of nannies to get our kids to and from school and care for them until we finally made it home each night.

But what I disliked the most was how little control I had over my own schedule. My deadlines were rigid, and I was generally required to do all my work at the office. I really didn't have a problem with taking on more responsibility, and I didn't mind working very hard or even working long hours. But while I was constantly forced to accommodate the company's schedule; the company never seemed interested in accommodating mine.

If my children had a one-hour elementary school show, I had

to waste an entire, precious vacation day, instead of just working from home or coming in a little late. Even if I got all my work done for the week, I was still expected to put in my forty, sixty or even eighty hours in the office. Complete availability to the company—in addition to productivity—was how you showed you were serious about your job and about getting ahead.

All the industries I worked in were very competitive, so I knew that if I wasn't willing to do it, they would find someone else who was. The veiled threat that I was replaceable lurked in the background of every job-related decision I made. I concluded that the corporate world was a "take it or leave it" proposition, and by 2005, I was ready to leave it.

This doesn't mean that corporate America can't be the right fit for some people, including people with families. And some companies are learning to offer more flexibility to their employees, especially now that millennials are in the workforce. But back when I was working for others, no one cared if I was happy or fulfilled. When I explained to one of my nicest bosses that I wasn't having much fun in my current position, he laughed and explained, "That's why they call it work!" Given our options at the time, Louis and I decided it was time to try something different.

As you will see in the pages that follow, we did learn a lot of valuable lessons and developed many important skills while working for large, successful companies. Perhaps more than anything, we both got a good look at what a well-run organization looks like from the inside. We knew how things were supposed to work, even if we didn't yet understand every little detail of how to get them to work that way. We also knew that—with the right strategy and execution—you could grow a company to become a dominant force in your market.

Leaving corporate America was the biggest risk we had ever taken as a couple. As we'll explain in the next chapter, we sank almost everything we had into our decision to become entrepreneurs. But, thanks to a lot of hard work and many strategy sessions in the hot tub, it has proven to be one of the most rewarding choices we have ever made.

CHAPTER 2

· · · · · · · · · · · · · · · · · ·

BUYING ONE HORN

BUYING ONE HORN

Many entrepreneurs are inspired to develop a product, service or innovation, and then start a business based on their new idea. Cheryl and I had almost the opposite experience. We made the decision to become entrepreneurs before we knew exactly what we wanted to sell.

Like Cheryl, I started out on the corporate path. After graduating with an engineering degree from McGill University in Montreal, I got a job building power plants for the local utility company. I also got a Master in Computer Architecture. To continue to advance, I was then faced with the choice of getting a Ph.D. or an MBA. I opted for an MBA at HEC in Paris (the French Harvard), where I met a very cute girl who, turned out to be Cheryl.

During our years in Paris, I followed one of the other traditional MBA paths, management consulting, where I would leave Cheryl every Sunday night to visit clients in other European cities, and then return home for the weekends. It was a tough life for newlyweds, but Cheryl was working long hours as well, so it was almost the same as if we were in the same city. Despite the hectic schedule, I did gain a strong foundation in business strategy and process reengineering, which helped us later on.

After we came to the United States, I worked for a nationwide armored car company, where I was eventually in charge of over 750 employees. It was here that I developed a knowledge of trucking and transportation, a taste for running a business, and a distaste for working for other people. Like my wife, I didn't mind working hard, but I was tired of having my schedule dictated to me for reasons that sometimes felt arbitrary or even obnoxious.

Fortunately, we were both tiring of our careers at the same time. Employing our "Triple-A Method", we analyzed our situation, identifying that we wanted more freedom and control over our lives. Part of our analysis was reading *The Millionaire Next Door* by Thomas Stanley and William Danko. At that point, we realized that the simplest path to the life we wanted—a life where we could set our own priorities—was entrepreneurship.

Choosing Our New Business

Once we decided to buy a business, we assessed our options, deliberating for a while about whether we would pursue Cheryl's line of expertise—the marketing of consumer packaged goods—or mine, which was trucking and transportation. In the end, we decided that the consumer goods market was already pretty crowded and would be difficult to break into. We briefly considered using our collective business experience in marketing, strategy, and process reengineering to open a consultancy, but we decided against it.

During one of our famous hot tub conferences, we learned from friends that most consultancies are not easily scalable; the client is buying your expertise, so the primary way to make more money is to work more hours. We wanted a business where we could increase our income without necessarily extending the hours we put in. In fact, our long-term plan was to hire other people to handle some of the day-to-day details of the business, to free up our schedules even more.

In the end, we decided on trucking and transportation, because we knew it could be scaled up over time. Another key reason we chose trucking is that we were taking out a large loan to make this purchase. To be considered credible borrowers, we had to demonstrate a level of knowledge of the industry.

After reviewing about fifty companies, we signed a non-disclosure agreement (NDA) with a local trucking company and began evaluating its financial records. The books had not been kept very carefully, but as we examined them we could see that there was potential for profit. After a few delays in the negotiating process, we acted and were ready to jump in.

In a very practical sense, we bought the assets of the company—including a fleet of trucks—which were not owned outright. This meant that we were assuming loan payments as well as paying the owner. In an acquisition, it is very important to buy the assets instead of buying the stock, because stock includes all the company's liabilities. (You don't want to spend your first days as an entrepreneur defending yourself in court against a wrongful termination suit related to the previous owner.) So with a few strokes of a pen, we were not only entrepreneurs, we were also deeply in debt!

Mitigating Risk

Buying One Horn Trucking was a huge risk. We took out a second mortgage on our home and put in almost all the cash we had saved over the years. But we made this decision with our eyes wide open. We knew how many businesses failed because of changes in the market or in the economy that were completely out of anyone's control. We also knew that plenty of would-be entrepreneurs overpay for a business and end up going bankrupt.

So we took many important steps to mitigate the risk. First, we opted for an owner-financed deal. This meant that we paid the owner over a period of time, contingent on the business's success. This essentially made us a partner with the owner (we actually retained him for a period of time as a paid consultant). It prevented him from getting us to overpay and then disappearing with our money.

Put in the plainest terms, if an owner convinces you that his business will generate a million dollars in profit each year, then it may be reasonable to pay him $5 million for it. But once he has his $5 million, he can easily skip town and leave you to deal with profits substantially lower than what he promised. In an owner-financed deal, he won't get his $5 million unless the business performs the way he promised over a period of time after the purchase. Naturally, this makes for a much more positive buying experience.

In addition to pursuing an owner-financed deal, we sought to expand what we could offer customers right away. A month after we bought One Horn Trucking, we started One Horn Transportation, a brokerage that enabled us to subcontract loads to outside trucking companies if we ran out of trucks to do the job ourselves. This also opened the door to service some customers that were farther away from our headquarters.

Another way we mitigated our risk was by having Cheryl continue to work at her corporate job for the first few months we owned One Horn, and then switch to part time for a few months after that. This ensured our personal income remained at a manageable level during the transition, but it certainly involved some late nights and long hours.

We also cut back on our personal expenses, which meant giving up our season tickets to the opera and the ballet in New York. We started budgeting a lot more carefully for our regular purchases, and took more modest vacations, or none at all. We did not change our children's activities—fortunately, soccer isn't as expensive as The Met—but those were still difficult times that we sometimes refer to as the "lean years."

Going All In: Challenges and Solutions

"At what point do you just close shop and walk away?"

Those were the words of an investment banker friend of ours who knew the sacrifices we were making to run our business during the early days. He didn't understand that we had no choice but to succeed. When a billion dollar company closes shop, everyone who works there moves on, and the bank is left to pick up the pieces. But if we had closed One Horn during the lean years, we would have lost our house, our savings, and been left with crushing personal debt.

We had gone "all in" with One Horn and had nothing to fall back on. That kind of commitment—scary as it is—has a powerful way of focusing the mind. It gave us the motivation we needed to weather the short-term trials involved in getting the business off the ground in order to reap the benefits later on.

So why were we having such a hard time? Our initial struggles were not due to any mistakes in our assessment of the business.

Our monthly expenditures were less than what our customers agreed to pay for our services, so we should have been profitable. The problem was that our profits were contingent on our trucks being on the road all month and our customers paying on time. We soon discovered that some of our customers didn't pay unless we spent a great deal of time and energy reminding them. Much to her dismay, I even had Cheryl start calling ahead of their payment due dates, a practice that would have never occurred to either of us before we got into the business.

Keeping the trucks on the road could be a challenge too. We had to get enough shipping customers, who often came from brokerages that then cut into our profits. Trucks had mechanical problems, and drivers got sick. Sometimes our owner-operators didn't manage their own resources as carefully as they should have, and needed advances on their weekly payments in order to complete a delivery. We ended up having to help them, because if the customer was deprived of service, our company's reputation would suffer. This put financial pressure on us at both ends of the process.

So for about three years, our lives were very stressful. We had to watch our bank accounts very closely to make sure certain checks had cleared when our balances were very low. It was absolutely vital that we never bounced checks or overdraw our accounts, because any damage to our credit would make carriers (outside trucking companies) unwilling to work with us on the brokerage side.

This meant that we sometimes had to take cash advances out on credit cards to ensure everyone was paid and our accounts stayed in the black. We were extremely fortunate to have allies at the bank who occasionally cleared certain checks from major companies quickly so that we wouldn't have to borrow more than was absolutely necessary. (We'll talk about how we learned to establish and maintain business credit in much more detail in Chapter 16, "Managing Business Credit.")

One benefit of these difficult years was that we learned to pay careful attention to the cash flow and efficiency of the business. This remains vital to long term growth and success. Many potentially profitable businesses are crippled by untold amounts of capital leaking out of inefficient and poorly monitored systems. After a while, we did build up enough cash reserves to sleep a little better at night. But we were still working a lot more than we wanted to work.

There were two more important takeaways from those lean years. The first was that—despite the stress—we still achieved our primary goal, which was to spend more time together as a family. The children were still playing sports and living the kind of lives we wanted for them. Even carrying balances on credit cards and obsessively watching accounts were completely worth being able to avoid the commute and have some control over our schedules.

The second is that we learned that the trucking business was not as straightforward as we had thought. There was a lot more to it than waking up every day and sending our employees to pick up loads in one place and deliver them somewhere else. The process was extremely complicated with many moving parts. And we soon began to realize that we were much better at some of those parts than others. In the next chapter we'll explain how we restructured the business around our strengths.

CHAPTER 3

· · · · · · · · · · · · · · · ·

A TALE OF TWO COMPANIES

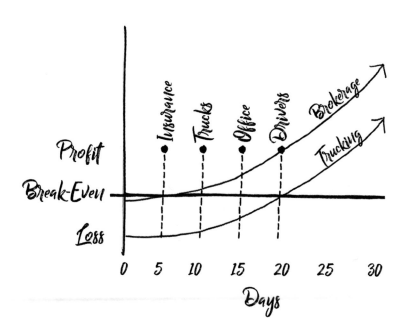

No one sets out to buy a business right before a recession. But in 2007—a little more than two years after Louis and I sank everything we had into One Horn—the economy took a significant turn for the worse. Ours was one of countless businesses affected.

The recession hit us particularly hard because our overhead costs were largely fixed. Like a restaurant that has to pay for rent, equipment, food, and salaries before it sells a single meal, we had to pay the salaries of our employees and make the payments on our tractors and trailers before we shipped a single load. Our analysis of our monthly expenses revealed that we did not actually break even until all our trucks had been on the road for 20 days. As rates started to decline, that left us just a couple of days (without holidays or bad weather) to try to pay ourselves.

And then we still needed reserves to cover any nonpayment by a customer or an unexpected expense like a truck breaking down. This meant not only the cost for repairs, but also lost revenue from deliveries that could not be made. We were frustrated and exhausted, but we refused to look back. We were determined to keep the hard-won freedom we did have and to fight for it even more.

The Pivot: Unleashing Profit and Opportunity

During one of our famous hot tub meetings, we had an important realization, and actually created a PowerPoint presentation entitled "Trucking Is Bad, Brokerage Is Good" (the analysis phase of our "Triple-A Method"). The aspect of our business that was profitable was the brokerage: getting new customers, scheduling their shipments using other trucking companies, and ensuring everything went smoothly. The part that was costing us our profits and peace of mind was the trucking itself: paying for and maintaining a fleet of trucks and paying the salaries of the drivers.

We assessed our options: What if we could restructure our business so that we were only a brokerage? What if we could get rid of the trucks and work with drivers as independent contractors instead of full time employees? Suddenly, the business seemed manageable again; most of our fixed costs—equipment payments, insurance, and salaries—would be gone. They would instead vary with the amount of work we actually did.

The pivot from being a trucking company to being a brokerage made all the sense in the world. It was not an easy transition, but we acted nonetheless. We offered each of our fulltime drivers the opportunity to purchase his truck from us, in effect enabling every driver to go into business for himself. However, none of them accepted the offer. We retained our fulltime office employee as long as we could, even trying to get her into sales for a while. But several months later, we just didn't have enough work for her, and so we had to let her go.

This was a very painful process, because we felt responsible for our full-time employees. We knew their spouses, their kids and their needs. In the end, we tried to be as upfront and honest as possible with them, to give them plenty of warning, and to retain them as long as we reasonably could. Ultimately, they understood the situation we were in, and I think they all felt we were fair.

We began to sell off all our assets, relieving us of mountains of debt and the monthly expenses associated with it. Thankfully, we did this before many of our huge competitors sold off their fleets, so we were able to recuperate a good portion of our acquisition costs. It was very reassuring to discover that we were actually ahead of the curve when we read the annual report of JB Hunt, and learned they had done the same thing six months after we divested our assets.

Even though this was a step forward in terms of our personal goals, it did feel like a step back. We sold our assets long before they had paid for themselves. In essence, we bought a trucking company and then shut it down. But given our situation, it was necessary to cut our losses in order to achieve what we wanted, which was total business freedom.

The Benefits

There were at least four immediate benefits we experienced as a result of our pivot from an asset-based company to a brokerage. First, the problem of fixed costs was all but eliminated. No longer did we have to pay for drivers, loans, insurance, and repairs regardless of whether or not we had business. We still had to go out and get customers, but we only incurred expenses when we actually did work.

Second, we also got rid of our office and began working from home. Before the advent of the Cloud, Louis created a virtual workspace that enabled our support staff to work from home as well. This not only reduced our expenses further, but it also enabled us to spend even more time with our kids. I was able to pick them up at school and even take them with me to run errands in the afternoon. I loved getting the chance to hear about their days and just enjoy their company.

The third benefit to becoming a brokerage was that we were no longer limited in the geographical areas we could service. In our previous asset-based model, we had to hire more drivers and buy more trucks in order to expand, greatly increasing our expense and risk. In our brokerage model, we were able to expand simply by finding new trucking companies in different parts of the country and Canada with whom we could contract. We were not responsible for the livelihood of our drivers anymore. This meant we could "bring on" new people without having to supply them with a full-time work. We became just one of their sources of work and income, which was a huge relief.

Fourth, we were able to become much more discriminating in the jobs we took. When we had fixed expenses, we had to take jobs that were not necessarily that profitable or convenient, simply to cover our monthly expenses. Now we could take only the jobs that made the most sense for our company. We were also no longer splitting our trucking margins with brokers, so this increased profitability as well. (Naturally, if we had a loyal customer who needed a job done that was less than perfect for us, we would always be happy to take one for the team.)

We were now in a fundamentally different business. Instead of loading trucks and making shipments mainly from New Jersey, we were matching good shippers with good carriers all over the country and in and out of Canada. At the end of the day, instead of working for twenty days each month to break even, we were meeting our expenses within a few days. And as you can imagine, we started sleeping much better at night.

The Not-So-Good News

There were challenges to our new model of business as well. First, we did not necessarily want new clients to know that we were working out of our home. This was at a time when working from home was not at all common. Once we had successfully completed work for them—and they knew that we were available to them whenever they needed us—it wasn't something we tried to conceal. But we knew that newer clients might not understand that we could provide high-quality service even without a big office.

We dealt with this by renting a box at the local UPS Store. This gave us a street address that could receive and sign for packages and would hold and deliver our business mail to us if we were out of town. These were significant advantages over just a post office box.

Working from home also had other challenges. Both Louis and I have always been able to discipline ourselves to be productive regardless of the environment, but we did decide to have separate home offices, mine on the first floor and his in the basement. As a coder, Louis was used to spending all day by himself, focused on programming. I am a much more social person, so I did miss the human interaction of a traditional office environment. Oftentimes, I called a good friend of mine—who was also working from home—and bounced ideas off her that I normally would have discussed at the office. I was also part of three different local entrepreneurial groups that met regularly in our region.

Perhaps the most significant challenge we encountered was that our company was no longer eligible for certain jobs because we were a brokerage, not asset based. Some government entities and large corporations, we learned, wrote their shipping contracts to work with carriers, not brokerages. We'll talk more about how we coped with this challenge in the next chapter.

Better Together: Dividing Responsibilities

We continued to divide the workload of the business based on our individual strengths and weaknesses. I am the more organized one, so I handled the bill payments, collections, banking, and calls when necessary. But, as Louis will explain in the next chapter, as the extrovert, my real focus was marketing and sales strategy, which included everything from cold calling and meeting with potential customers, to creating and managing the website.

Louis handled the actual dispatches, sold off the equipment, and also leveraged his technology skills by focusing on the computer programming side. This involved building our software package—Stratebo—and ultimately preparing us for growth. (See the next chapter for details on Stratebo and other growth-based projects.) He also handled insurance, Department of Transportation compliance, and any tax issues. (On that front, he got the short end of the stick.)

Still, as with anything in life, there are certain tasks no one wants to do. We would typically divide these between us, but we would also periodically reexamine them to see if we could eliminate them altogether. For example, neither of us particularly relished the afternoon bank run we had to make each day, but eventually we got a check scanner from our bank to avoid the trip. We'll talk more about the ways we were able to automate certain tasks in Chapter 10, "Automate It!"

By transforming our trucking company into a brokerage, we gained greater peace of mind and freedom. The lean years were just about over. In the next chapter, Louis will explain how we went from just making ends meet to growing our revenue and greatly increasing our profitability.

CHAPTER 4

· · · · · · · · · · · · · · · · · · ·

FROM SURVIVING TO THRIVING

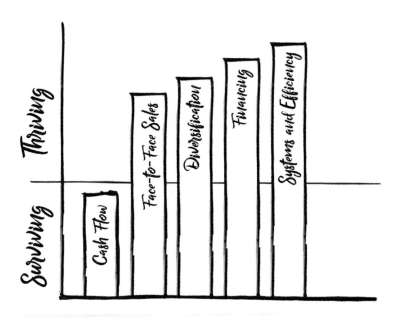

"**L**et me make some calls," I told the irate customer over the phone, while I signaled to Cheryl that I had the situation under control. I called our driver and found out that he had had some equipment problems and was delayed by an hour. Fortunately, the driver was only a few minutes away from the customer when we spoke, so the situation was resolved relatively quickly.

About a month later I went to see the customer, "Greg," in person to discuss the mishap. He understood that things like this happen in the shipping world, and he agreed that we had answered his call promptly and dealt with the situation as best as anyone could have. But he still seemed discontent about something, so I tried to keep him talking to discover what it was.

"Louis, where exactly were you when you took my call last month?" Greg finally asked.

"Well," I replied a little sheepishly, "I have to confess, I was in a chairlift on a ski slope in Europe."

"I knew it!" Greg exclaimed with laugh. "I knew you were somewhere having fun with your family. But you did everything I needed you to do. I've been in business for thirty years, and I'm still chained to my desk."

This was what Cheryl and I had been after all along. We wanted to live our lives our own way, without being prisoners in our offices all week. We had taken a huge risk and had put in a lot of hard work, but it was finally starting to pay off.

Preparing for Growth

We were staying afloat in the recession, but we wanted to move beyond mere survival. We needed to expand our business in order to make progress on our debts, but we had to do so without spending all the extra income on salaries. The answer was to increase our efficiency, so we could do more in fewer hours, and to perfect our sales and marketing strategy, so we could attract the best possible customers.

Improved efficiency was key to increasing our freedom even as we grew. Even though we had gotten rid of all our trucks, I still had to be available to our customers around the clock if a new order came in, or if something went wrong with a delivery. Yet I knew there were ways I could automate some of these tasks so I could get customers the information they needed without responding individually to each one.

Enhancing Our Software System

The software system we had purchased with One Horn was very inefficient, so I used my coding background to add features to the program. Each fix saved us a great deal of time. Eventually I began replacing entire portions of the system with my own programming, streamlining data entry, and enabling the system to respond automatically to new orders.

Modifying a software program you are actually using to run a business can feel a little like changing a tire on a car while it's moving. We did research other systems that we could have purchased to replace our system entirely, but we found that these were sold as services rather than products. Switching would have added thousands to our monthly expenses. In the long run, it was much more cost effective for me to create a new system that suited our needs and could be adapted as those needs changed.

Creating this new system—which we named Stratebo—was vital for us to grow our business without working more hours or hiring too many employees. (I originally named the system OHLALA, which I thought it gave it a French air of *je ne sais quoi*, but in the end we decided it was not "manly enough" for the trucking business.) Early on I focused the development design towards making the system fast for the user, so we could manage more loads per person than the other software out there. Often this was not too difficult, since some of our competitors still use AS/400 type systems (think blue screen monitors used in movies in the 80's). This was just another way we learned to leverage our strengths as we continued on our entrepreneurial journey.

Expanding and Diversifying Our Customer Base

Cheryl's strong marketing background made her a natural choice as the face of One Horn. Despite little experience with sales, she approached large corporations for business with great determination. Marketing and sales—although sometimes discussed interchangeably—are quite different activities. The first focuses on brand awareness and name recognition, while the second works on closing the deal with actual customers.

Sales as an entrepreneur was very different from marketing

for a large, well known corporation. A friend of ours zeroed in on the shift Cheryl needed to make right away. He told her that she wasn't hungry like an entrepreneur has to be in order to keep the company going. In corporate marketing, you can have a campaign that doesn't quite achieve its goals, you adjust next time and life goes on. When selling for your own company, closing the deal today carries a great deal more urgency.

True to her tireless work ethic, Cheryl read books and went to seminars on sales to train for her new role. She then set her schedule, prepared her scripts, and forced herself to cold call for a block of time each day. She called this her "Power Hour," which actually often lasted two or three hours. Cheryl stuck with it even though it was hard not to take all the rejections personally. ("What? You mean you don't want to use our services???") And like all good salespeople, she started to develop thicker skin.

We soon found that Cheryl had a lot more success with face-to-face meetings than with cold calls, direct mail, and other approaches. We also discovered that our industry required her to adjust her presentation style. Cheryl was used to putting on a suit, entering a boardroom full of executives, and firing up a well-prepared PowerPoint presentation. That didn't go over as well in a sweltering warehouse full of workers. So she soon learned to dress more casually, present our business in the conversational language with which our potential customers were more comfortable, and leave them with a succinct one-pager explaining who we were and what we did.

Cheryl, who is African American, also bought 1 percent of the company from me, so she would own 51 percent of the business, and we could get certified as a Minority Business Enterprise (MBE) and a Woman Business Enterprise (WBE). We did this with an eye toward government contracts and corporations that cared about vendor diversity. This was a lengthy, complicated process. But once it was complete, we just had to focus on networking, which was one of Cheryl's strengths.

We also worked to diversify our customer base. When we were running One Horn Trucking, we were shipping mostly construction materials and equipment. That meant that when construction slowed during the recession, we were hit particularly hard. We started looking for customers whose markets were growing at the time, as well as those whose loads had to ship regardless of economic conditions. We began to ship for customers building cellphone towers, as well as for solar, wind, and other sustainable energy firms. We didn't end up signing long-term customers in all these industries, but we learned a lot in the process.

Refining our Client Base

As we mentioned in the last chapter, our bids to ship for government entities got off to a very disappointing start. Cheryl had great success networking with decision makers, but after months of cultivating relationships and building trust, we learned that many had to sign contracts with asset-based carriers instead of trucking brokers like One Horn. The same was true of some large corporations that had the capacity to manage individual carriers. They often didn't see the value of employing a brokerage, and their legal departments typically didn't want to deal with the nuances of writing a contract for an entity that didn't actually own the trucks.

We had moments when we second-guessed our decision to sell all our assets, but we continued to press forward. We began to focus more on local small to mid-sized, privately owned companies, where Cheryl could continue to meet with decision makers in person. We also learned to ask right away if the company had a legal department and if they had a contract designed for brokers or carriers.

These experiences taught us to determine quickly if someone would be a good client or not, so that we did not waste time cultivating a relationship that wouldn't go anywhere. At the same time, it helped us discover that there were some corporations that understood how brokerages worked and were happy to sign contracts with us. We also learned to determine whether or not a customer paid its bills and paid on time before we would do business with them. This would prove vital to our later expansion.

Despite a few setbacks, we were beginning to thrive. By trying everything that we could think of, evaluating, continuing what worked, and discontinuing what didn't, we had built a profitable business in the middle of a recession. We were making progress on our debts, while gaining control over our schedules and our priorities.

Although we were free from our largest financial anxieties, friends would occasionally ask if we missed our "safe" corporate jobs. We always answered "no." The auspiciousness of our choice was brought home to me when I bumped into an old colleague from the armored car company I worked for before we became entrepreneurs. We chatted for a bit, and he remarked that the entire corporate management team—all the way up to the chairman—had been replaced. The "safe" job I had left hadn't been so safe after all.

CHAPTER 5

· · · · · · · · · · · · · · · · ·

BUILDING THE
FREIGHT AGENT MODEL

When Dick Fosbury won the gold medal in the high jump in the 1968 Olympics, he not only set an Olympic Record, but he also changed the sport forever. Before 1968, athletes favored the straddle technique or the Western Roll, clearing the bar either feet or hips first. Fosbury approached the jump in a completely new way—dubbed the Fosbury Flop—by clearing the bar head first, or "backwards" in the eyes of spectators. Today, virtually all high jumpers at every level of the sport use Fosbury's technique.

Sometimes it takes a radical reimagining of what you are doing to get the results you seek. Louis and I had made tremendous progress toward our goals of both profitability and greater freedom by switching to a brokerage and significantly diversifying our customer base. The economy seemed to be headed toward recovery, so we began to investigate what we could do to grow even more.

During this time, we attended an event with the Wharton Club of New Jersey, led by Solange Perret. Her presentation included a powerful illustration of the need to produce a Fosbury-like innovation in order to achieve the results we wanted. Particularly as we considered how long it took me to cultivate and sign a new customer. Using our Triple-A Method, before: we realized that to increase our growth potential, we would have to do something profoundly different.

Exponential Growth

The desire for exponential—instead of just linear—growth

led us to adopt the Freight Agent Model (FAM) of business. Rather than just hiring truckers and matching them with shippers, we began to hire freight agents. These are independent contractors who have their own "book of business," or roster of customers whom they service on a regular basis.

In the FAM, the agents bring in the business by establishing relationships with companies that want to ship their goods. They then hire outside trucking companies to haul the loads, and we, as the brokerage, handle the financing and back office responsibilities. Suddenly I was free from sales and business development, and Louis was free from assigning the loads to trucking companies and monitoring the progress of deliveries. The only downside was that we had to split the commission with the agent, but we soon learned that it's much better to get 30 percent of a huge pie rather than 100 percent of a small pie.

We were now offering our customers—both the freight agents and the shippers—the service we were best at providing: financial stability and security. The agents handled sales and shipping logistics, and we handled the money exchange. We made sure the truckers were paid promptly and we took care of billing the shippers.

Of course we also absorbed some of the risk; if a shipper didn't pay, we would lose the money. However, we had already learned how to screen customers very well. By declining to work with those who didn't pay within thirty days (which a quick credit check can verify), we were almost never stuck with customers who didn't pay at all.

Leveraging Reliability and Credit

Reliability and extended access to credit were critical to generating a new level of growth for One Horn. The trucking industry tracks brokerage payment patterns very closely and reports on what it finds. Agents whose brokerages are late just a couple of times could lose all their business in a matter of weeks, because the carriers would simply refuse to work with them. We were able to bring on a lot of agents who left other brokerages because they didn't pay as promptly as we did.

Because we had access to lines of credit that were not directly overseen by the bank, we could also offer our agents a lot more credit than they might get elsewhere. This enabled them to ship more loads with the assurance that their truckers would be paid on time. One of our agents was only able to get enough credit to cover ten loads at a time from his previous broker (to ship for a Fortune 500 company). Since he came on board with us, we have had times where we had close to 200 loads open in the receivable, and now both the agent and we are flourishing as a result.

As we developed a reputation for extending larger lines of credit and paying promptly, our business began to grow exponentially, while still increasing our personal freedom. Under our old model, it would take me several months to generate a few hundred thousand dollars of business. Now we could interview an agent, persuade him to come over to our brokerage, and he would begin generating that level of business within a few days or even hours.

The biggest challenge with the transition was getting our first agent on board, because we didn't yet have an established track record. On the advice of colleagues, we created a position description and retained a headhunter, with mixed results. In addition to the retainer, the headhunter was promised a commission based on the volume of business of each agent we hired. Unfortunately, we soon discovered that she was encouraging the agents she was interviewing to exaggerate their books of business in order to inflate her commission.

In the end, we did glean some value from the headhunter, despite her dishonesty. When we informed her that we wanted to cancel our recruiting contract, she refused to return her retainer. So instead, we used her to hire a back office employee, which we desperately needed to help service our growing post-recession house accounts, as well as that person's colleague, an agent with a very small book of business.

Recruiting Through Innovation

By pivoting to an agent-based brokerage, Louis and I found our own daily tasks changing once again. Louis was able to modify our existing software to handle the new commission structure and ensure everything was tracked and paid on time. I shifted from sales and marketing to recruiting more agents.

To do this, I joined an industry organization to learn from people who had used the same model. I soon found that recruiting agents was a better fit for me than sales had been. I'm very passionate about our company and our values, so it was easy to talk to agents about what we had to offer.

Recruiting involved a lot of marketing; to get agents interested, we needed name recognition and brand awareness. We started by advertising on some of the logistics websites that had job postings, and after attending some business seminars, I also began to utilize social media. Using social media this way was relatively new at the time (more about this in Chapter 12, "The Marketing Triad: Social Media, Publishing, and Awards"), and we were very fortunate to have the opportunity to own the social media footprint for a transportation brokerage.

So I built a mini-website that described our program for freight agents. I also started blogging and participating in LinkedIn conversations. This really got our name out and drove more traffic to our website. One agent saw the ad, went to our website, clicked on the leaders' page, and saw my picture. He recognized me from a LinkedIn conversation and decided to give us chance. Within months, he had become one of our best agents, and I knew our social media program was working.

The recruiting process also drove our internal innovation. Every time we brought in new agents, we sat down with them to learn what they felt they needed to be successful. For example, when we brought on agents shipping for the food industry, we learned we needed to be able to issue checks to drivers remotely so they could pay people to unload their trucks. Gradually, we adjusted and perfected our systems and processes to ensure they remained efficient while maintaining our control over credit and cash flow.

Louis also began refining our software system so that others could use it. As we mentioned in the last chapter, all the software packages sold for our industry were very expensive to purchase and maintain. Having Louis do the programming for One Horn enabled us to upgrade on our own and ensure the system kept up with our agents' needs while saving significant cash outlays.

Thanks to our agent-based model, we were able to expand the number of industries we serviced, again protecting ourselves from a slowdown in one particular area. We started out in flatbed and overdimensional transportation, but soon included dry van and finally temperature-controlled trailers. We learned about each industry's unique risks and challenges and how to steer away from freight that didn't work for us, further refining our customer base.

Expansion Challenges

We faced two major challenges as we expanded. The first was that each time we hired more agents, we had to be able to access more credit. In the end, we were actually able to get banks to compete to lend to us, even in the middle of a global recession. We'll talk about more how we did this in Chapter 16, "Managing Business Credit."

The second challenge was that we could no longer interview everyone in person. Although we still met with individuals within a certain geographic radius, it simply wasn't practical to fly all over the country for the rest. Ultimately, we had to become much better at assessing an agent's book of business, industry knowledge, level of honesty and integrity, and how well he or she would fit into our corporate culture over the phone.

The unexpected benefit was that we got a good snapshot

of the agents' professionalism. Since many agents establish relationships with their own customers over the phone, the process gave us the opportunity to assess their communication skills. (Still we always took other steps to verify their books of business as well.) In the end, our first hire became just one of many fruitful professional relationships established without an in-person meeting.

Shifting to the FAM enabled us both to grow our business exponentially and to gain more freedom than ever before. Louis still keeps his phone by the bedside, but he hasn't had to answer it in four or five years. I was freed from selling to shippers and recruiting truckers, so I was able to do more of what I loved. We were spending less time working "in" our business and more time working "on" our business, as author of *The E-Myth Revisited*, Michael Gerber, would say. In the next chapter we'll explain the steps we took to make that business scalable.

CHAPTER 6

. . . .

CREATING A
SCALABLE MODEL

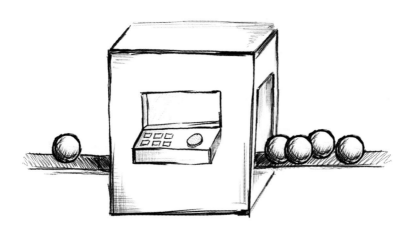

In late October 2012, Hurricane Sandy swept across the mid-Atlantic, causing billions of dollars of damage and leaving millions without electricity. Although Cheryl and I were spared significant losses, our house—which was also the headquarters of One Horn— was without power for four and a half days. Considering we ran the whole company from our computers, this could have spelled disaster.

Thankfully, I had proactively moved all our servers into the cloud, knowing that our agents from all over the country needed to be able to access our system at all times. A catastrophe like Hurricane Sandy was a serious test of how well this precaution would work. Could we keep the company running even as we waited in endless lines to buy gas for our generator?

Fortunately, the rest of the company felt absolutely no ill-effects of our power outage. We were able to use a cellphone as a hot spot to stay connected on our computers, and it was business as usual for everyone else who was out of the path of the storm. Moving our system to the cloud was just one of many steps we took to ensure that One Horn could operate smoothly and easily even as we expanded.

Understanding Scalability

The scalability of a business relates to how easily it can be expanded. For example, suppose you have a doughnut shop working at full capacity and you want to double the number of doughnuts you produce and sell. You will most likely need twice as much equipment and workplace square footage, as well as twice as many employees and ingredients. Your business can be expanded, but your expenses will rise almost as quickly as your output.

The same is true of trucking. Once a trucking company is working at capacity, you basically have to double your trucks, drivers, insurance, and other expenditures in order to double your volume of business. In some industries, or under some circumstances, doubling your output may actually more than double your costs because of greater complexity and other regulations.

A more easily scalable business can be doubled without doubling every other expense. For example, if you have created a piece of software that you send to your customers by email, you can double, triple, or increase your customer base by a factor of 100 without increasing your costs much at all. You only have to account for the time needed to enter new email addresses, which you could have the customers do themselves. You will have growth in your support department, but that should not grow as fast as your volume—at least until you are quite large.

Of course most businesses can't be expanded that rapidly at that low a cost, but you can still work to increase your profit more quickly than your expenses and complexity. As an entrepreneur, you should regularly ask yourself if you can double your business without working twice as many hours. (This was one of the reasons we did not form a consultancy, as we mentioned in Chapter 2, "Buying One Horn.") If the answer is no, what are some steps you can take to change that?

CREATING A SCALABLE MODEL

The two basic factors limiting the growth of a business are time and money. Some aspects of expansion—like buying more trucks or doughnut-making equipment—require a substantial investment of capital. Other aspects—onboarding new employees, agents or customers, billing, dealing with increased regulations, and so on—require extra time. The key to scalability is to reduce the time and money involved in expansion.

Making One Horn Scalable

The key to making One Horn scalable was increasing the efficiency of our systems. In practical terms this meant programming Stratebo to do more of our work for us. The first year after we pivoted to the agent-based model of business, I spent thirty-five hours a week on billing. Today I spend about three hours a week on billing for a much larger volume of business, all because of improvements I programed into Stratebo. Ultimately, we were able to grow our business by a factor of ten while actually reducing the number of hours we put in.

As an agent-based broker, a huge part of our job was billing customers and cutting checks for truckers. Initially, Cheryl would enter all the carrier checks into the system individually. She would then print out our checks, sign them by hand, stuff them into envelopes and take them to the post office. (Eventually, we did get the kids to help with that!) Today, thanks to the modifications I made in Stratebo, Cheryl can do all this work with a few clicks of a button.

To expand One Horn, we also had to be able to screen and hire new agents. And as you might expect, the degree of our scalability depended on how quickly and efficiently we could do this. Initially, setting up a new agent in the system required a huge number of entries, which could take four or five hours. But after once again writing an extra piece of software to automate the data entry, I was able to speed up this process considerably. Furthermore, adding a new customer now takes about five minutes, instead of an hour or more.

Several years ago, we had an interview with a new agent at 7:30 in the morning. He was ready to come on board, but we were headed to Panama on a 2:00 PM flight. By the time we left for the airport, we had conducted three sets of interviews, three reference checks, and gotten the guy in the system. By the time we landed in Panama, he had already generated revenue for the company!

Streamlining the Hiring Process

Our hiring process wasn't always that easy. When we first began hiring agents, we rushed through the interviews and reference checks, and brought them on a little too quickly. Then we began to learn firsthand the cost of a bad hire. We had a customer in Florida who didn't pay; he actually disappeared on us and then declared bankruptcy. Then the agent who had brought us the customer disappeared, because she had known the customer wasn't going to pay. Our company lost the money, and we learned a very hard lesson.

As a transportation brokerage, hiring an unscrupulous agent who did not treat his truckers well could reflect very badly on us, even if we paid on time. And of course, an agent who knowingly brought us non-paying customers like the one in Florida would cost us a great deal of money. So we started to be a lot more careful, which made the hiring process take a lot longer.

Initially, we had Cheryl talk with prospective agents first; their second interview would be with a member of our staff, and the third would be with me. But we soon found that this system was wasting a lot of Cheryl's time with unqualified candidates. It might take an hour to uncover a clear sign that the person was not right for our company. One candidate actually revealed to Cheryl—well into her interview—that she didn't have a cell phone, because she "never left her house!"

After some trial and error, we developed a list of initial screening questions to go through with all candidates. We also signaled during the initial interview that we were very serious about performing reference checks, also known as TORC (Threat of Reference Check), a term coined by Brad Smart, author of *Topgrading*. (Some candidates would simply disappear once they learned we were actually going to call their references, a far cry from our experiences in corporate America!) Doing this early on let us know whether it was even worth our time to do a second interview.

Once our employee did the initial screening interview, Cheryl repeated the screening questions and then interviewed the candidate to determine if he or she would fit with our company's culture and values. We wanted people who were honest, reliable and responsive, and treated truckers and shippers with respect. Once she knew a candidate was qualified, Cheryl became very good at weeding out the agents who were just good actors. Then

I would interview for industry and technical skills. Finally, we had developed a hiring process that was both thorough and efficient.

Rather than micromanage everyone, we choose to hire honest agents and give them a lot of autonomy. Our system is very good at monitoring cash flow and catching problems quickly, so there is very little chance we will lose a large enough amount of money to cause us real problems. (We'll talk more about this in Chapter 15, "Treasury Management: How We Manage Cash Flow...Daily.") We've been able to onboard new agents quickly, and incidents like the one with the customer from Florida have become extremely rare.

Ultimately, One Horn has become increasingly scalable because we have accelerated the automation of the business faster than we've grown. The amount of time we spend on financial transactions has almost nothing to do with the volume of business that we do in a day. We could double or triple our business tomorrow, without spending any more time in the office.

Our top-of-the-line automation has also made life easier for our agents. We have been able to tremendously reduce the amount of time they have to spend entering information into the system, so everyone wins. In the next chapter, we'll talk about an exciting new model that makes the benefits of this automation available to a much broader customer base.

CHAPTER 7

. . . .

BLUE OCEAN: THE BIRTH OF
THE CORPORATE AGENT MODEL

As the old saying goes, timing is everything. When Cheryl and I initially pivoted to the agent-based brokerage model, nationwide financial turmoil was forcing a lot of brokerages out of business. The freight agents who worked for those troubled companies were looking for new employment opportunities, so we were able to hire many of them. But like any trend—in a specific industry or in the economy as a whole—it didn't last forever.

When the market was flooded with agents looking for work, we could merely advertise on industry websites—as well as promote ourselves on social media—and the agents would find us. But once the weaker brokerages either closed their doors or were acquired by other firms, most agents settled down with stable companies. This made recruiting a much bigger challenge.

Happily employed agents need much greater incentives to switch brokerages, because such changes involve significant risk. To move their transactions to another brokerage, they have to persuade their shipping clients to move with them. Some shippers might be tempted to take their business elsewhere, so unless an agent's current brokerage is really serving them poorly, there is very little reason to switch.

When we first started recruiting, the compensation program we offered was extremely competitive. As the market for agents got tighter, a lot of companies began to match what we offered. Then some really large companies started recruiting aggressively, offering signing bonuses and wild perks like free vacations to Las Vegas. Add to this the fact that there is no definitive industry list of freight agents. Bringing on new agents was starting to feel impossible.

President John F. Kennedy once said, "Change is the law of life." When things are going well—as they were for us when the market was flooded with agents—it is extremely tempting to assume that those economic conditions will remain forever. But reality never works like that. Leaders of successful companies accept and adjust to change, so we set out to adapt to this new market reality.

The Blue Ocean Strategy

In their 2005 book *Blue Ocean Strategy: How to Create Uncontested Market Space and Make the Competition Irrelevant,* authors W. Chan Kim and Renee Mauborgne demonstrate how hundreds of companies handled change by rising above the cutthroat competition in their industries. Rather than outperform their rivals to increase their share of existing demand, these companies succeeded in creating new demand, turning non-customers into customers.

Based on the terminology Kim and Mauborgne created, the freight brokerage industry had become a "red ocean," a marketspace defined by brutal competition and razor-thin profit margins. "Blue oceans," they explain, "...are defined by untapped marketspace, demand creation, and the opportunity for highly profitable growth. Although some blue oceans are created well beyond existing industry boundaries, most are created by expanding existing industry boundaries... In blue oceans, competition is irrelevant as the rules of the game are waiting to be set."

We needed to get out of the red ocean and create our own blue ocean, which in our case would be a new source of agents. Having analyzed the situation, we assessed our options. It dawned on me that there was a huge pool of potential agents that no one had yet tapped into: the shippers themselves. Most manufacturers were participating a great deal in the process of brokering their freight without necessarily realizing it. They just didn't have the tools to do everything on their own.

Just as there are now a plethora of websites that allow consumers to book their own flights and hotel rooms—effectively becoming their own travel agents—it dawned on me that we could use Stratebo to do the same for manufacturers. This realization led us to act and develop our Corporate Agent Program, which gives shippers the tools and training to broker their own freight. This can save them millions of dollars in agent fees and provides One Horn with our blue ocean of new agents.

Perhaps the most important aspect of this pivot for One Horn is that shippers are much easier to find than agents. We could target a particular industry, find a list of manufacturers and pursue them like any traditional sales initiative. In addition, the incentives for shippers to broker their freight with us are much better than they are for agents to switch. The service we offer will not only save them a great deal of money, it is also low risk to try and they can use it in combination with shipping agents.

Navigating a New Ocean

Any new business model requires many internal adjustments to make it work. Stratebo is easy to teach, but we quickly found that our success in creating corporate agents was largely dependent on how well they understood the transportation industry from the start. If they had been involved with the shipping process to begin with, they learned easily and took to the system at once. If they were not as closely involved, the training process could take a great deal longer.

The greatest potential problem we faced in our new marketspace was the fact that we could now be perceived as competing with our own agents for customers. We anticipated this problem and took immediate steps to ensure that our agents remained happy and felt that we were taking good care of them. We made an explicit commitment to them that if we crossed paths with one of their prospects or customers, we would not sign that customer as a corporate agent.

We also take other steps to ensure our current agents are thriving. In addition to monitoring morale in general, we watch their commissions very closely. Each week I produce a commission report. If they have a good week, we congratulate them and try to discover what may have led to their success. If they have a bad week, we offer sympathy and ask if there is anything we can do to help them perform better.

One of our agents went through a very challenging time during which she had to rebuild her customer base. We stuck by her and did all we could to help her reach new clients, and it was wonderful when she started to flourish. Both Cheryl and I are so happy to see her succeed, and she is grateful we were there for her when she needed us. Our genuine interest in the success of our agents is a vital part of our company culture.

One of the advantages to a family run business is that the bosses aren't nameless, faceless executives, or board members. We truly care about our agents and their families, and of course when our agents thrive, so do we. We know every industry has its highs and lows, but we do our best to offer personalized attention through it all. These kinds of relationships are what brought us success in the first place, and they are what will help us all thrive together regardless of what happens in our industry.

As of this writing, the Corporate Agent Model remains very much a work in progress. As with anything radically new, we are learning as we go. In the meantime, we are also working to diversify our family interests, which we'll discuss in the next chapter.

CHAPTER 8

· · · · · · · · · · · · · · · · · ·

DIVERSIFYING THE FAMILY INTERESTS

One Horn

LexaGen

Stratebo

Just like any financial advisor will tell you it's a good idea to diversify your investment portfolio, Louis and I knew it was important to diversify our family's sources of income. We know a lot of couples who do this by having one member run a business while the other works at a traditional job, just as we did when we first bought One Horn. This strategy helps families mitigate the risk of entrepreneurship; after all, a reliable salary can go a long way toward balancing out the ups and downs of running a business.

Although we went "all in" with One Horn when I quit my day job, we felt extremely vulnerable during the Great Recession. We were fully committed to make our company a success, but we also knew that—in the long run—it was probably not a good idea to keep all our eggs in one basket. Fortunately, as Louis improved Stratebo's capabilities, One Horn no longer required full-time hours from both of us to keep it running.

As Stratebo automated us out of the most aggravating parts of our day jobs, we began to consider what would be the best use of our extra time and energy (besides skiing!). Since there was no way either of us was going to return to a traditional work environment, we concluded that, in addition to exploring future pivots for One Horn, we would each run a separate business of our own.

LexaGen Freedom Accelerator

LexaGen Freedom Accelerator—a combination of our children's names—is my business growth coaching practice, which uses a model where I meet with my clients' full leadership teams on a monthly or quarterly basis. In many ways, it is also the culmination of my life's work. Using my MBA, my experience in corporate America, and my years of working to grow and scale One Horn, I am now able to help business owners get to freedom faster, whatever freedom means to them. As Simon Sinek, author of *Start with Why*, would put it, freedom is my "why," and I have found the same goes for a lot of my clients. I also believe that coaching business leaders and their teams is my calling; I find spending the day with a client team more enjoyable and energizing than any other work I have ever done.

As I'll discuss more in Chapter 12, "The Marketing Triad: Social Media, Publishing, and Awards," One Horn's tremendous growth led to opportunities for me to write, lead entrepreneurs' groups, and speak to various business audiences. As my articles became more widely circulated and I met people at various events, I would often get requests for mentorship, particularly from other female entrepreneurs. I enjoy giving back to others, and so as long as my schedule permitted I was happy to help.

As my children got older and began heading off to college, I naturally had a little more time on my hands. Employing our "Triple-A Method," I analyzed my situation, realizing I was also looking for more fulfillment in my life. Starting my own coaching practice seemed like a natural step as requests for my expertise increased and One Horn needed less of my attention. The more I thought about it, the more excited I was to help other entrepreneurs and business leaders achieve their goals and dreams.

As I assessed my options, rather than start from scratch, it made more sense for me to use a proven methodology, so I evaluated several different models. Then I acted and decided to become certified through Gazelles, a worldwide coaching association founded by Verne Harnish, author of *Mastering the Rockefeller Habits and Scaling Up*. (Harnish also founded EO (Entrepreneurs' Organization), of which both Louis and I are members.) This decision enabled me to take advantage of all the organization's curated content and gave me access to a community of fellow coaches across the country and the world. These, combined with my own education, business background, and entrepreneurial experience, have equipped me to help mid-market businesses reach and sustain their growth objectives.

The Gazelles model is a group coaching method in which coaches work with an organization's entire executive team to identify their organization's goals and determine the most effective path to achieve them. Gazelles coaches have their own clients, but we pool our wisdom and experience with the attitude that there is an abundance of work for all of us.

I start my clients out with a two-day planning session, during which we work on developing long term (ten to thirty year) goals, medium term (three to five year) goals, as well as clarifying purpose and core values. We then create their annual plan and begin to meet quarterly (or monthly, depending on the needs of the client) to discuss strategic planning, shorter term goals, hiring practices, leadership strategies, and so on. Not only do I help them grow and scale their businesses, I also teach them how to develop systems and create a culture of action and accountability so that the business doesn't constantly demand all their time and energy.

I have met many people who are experts on the technical side of their businesses, whether they are attorneys, manufacturers, or financial advisors. But this kind of knowledge doesn't necessarily translate into the ability to effectively run a law practice, a factory, or a financial firm. By helping them develop good systems and strong communication, they are able to create accountability for the organization's goals. When all the employees understand how their jobs contribute toward the overall goals of the company, they work with greater passion and purpose. This also helps to ensure that everyone will continue to advance the goals of the business, even if the owner isn't constantly around.

Mentoring other entrepreneurs has taught me that freedom means different things to different people. I have always defined freedom as the ability to do what I want, when I want to do it. For me, that meant things like spending time with my kids and going skiing with my family. For someone else it might mean more time to do charitable work, participate in a hobby, or care for an elderly parent. Of course, freedom often comes incrementally, like it did for Louis and me. For some clients, just being able to get away for one vacation a year is a huge step in the right direction. Others might be looking for the financial freedom to invest in a new product line or free their firm from debt.

Almost all industries today are extremely competitive, so running a business without consistent advice doesn't make much more sense than an athlete showing up to the Olympics without a coach. Louis and I have benefited immensely from coaches and advisors over the years, and we are grateful for the opportunity to give back to others.

Stratebo Technologies

As you know from reading the previous chapters, the software Louis built for One Horn has been the key to increasing our efficiency and productivity while reducing the amount of time and energy we have to invest in the business. From the beginning, it seemed obvious that all of the capabilities Louis was programming into the software would be useful to others. So we took steps several years ago to create a separate software development company.

Stratebo started as a side tool to ease some of the data entry tasks that were becoming tedious and time consuming. Over time the software (www.stratebo.com) gradually incorporated all the functionality that we were getting from other purchased software. Once all was integrated, the focus switched to reducing the effort needed for every task and increasing the number of shipments a single person could handle simultaneously. Our focus now is making the interface mostly disappear and having the software act as an intelligent assistant, dependable and always available from any device anywhere in the world.

Louis has successfully adapted the software to serve brokerages, transportation companies, and manufacturers, just to name a few. One of our more recent innovations is to make Stratebo mobile friendly, enabling our clients to run their businesses from their phones. Louis is also hard at work adding extra features that will meet the needs of companies in an even broader array of industries.

Stratebo is a classic example of how solving our own problems enabled us to solve problems for so many others. As we mentioned in Chapter 4, "From Surviving to Thriving," Louis was shocked to learn that one of Stratebo's top selling competitors still uses an AS/400-based system, the monochrome screen setup that dates all the way back to 1980s! While Stratebo has far more capabilities than these archaic systems, we have always strived to stay just below the "bleeding edge" of technology— the place where a technology is so new that it may be risky and expensive to implement. Instead, we offer our clients the newest reliable capabilities that will make them most competitive. And thanks to all of Louis's innovations, Stratebo can now help all kinds of companies streamline their accounting processes, keep careful track of where all their money is going, and serve their customers more efficiently.

Automation—like that provided by Stratebo—is the future of business, but it can be scary for owners or managers for a number of reasons. First, it's easy to be intimidated by new technology, even if it is easy to use. Second, most of us are at least somewhat resistant to change. We get used to doing things a certain way, and it is difficult to adapt, even if the new way is more efficient. It takes deliberate effort to prevent our business processes from getting stuck in a rut.

Third, many people are worried that automation will eliminate jobs. On a micro level this can be true. Automation currently enables us to run One Horn with basically no employees. However, in the grand scheme of things, automation doesn't necessarily eliminate jobs; it simply changes them. For example, many people were anxious that Automatic Teller Machines (ATMs)—which became more widespread in the 1980s—would eliminate the need for bank tellers. Instead, the hundreds of thousands of ATMs all over the country have coincided with an increase in demand for workers to maintain and repair the machines.

Still, the thought of laying off employees in the short term can be unpleasant. Mid-level managers may see their status as directly related to the number of people they oversee, which causes them to see automation as a demotion. Smaller businesses may employ family members, which makes the situation even more sensitive.

Louis and I look at the challenges of automation differently. In the long run, repetitive tasks that can be done by machine eventually will be. That is simply the way an efficient, competitive economy works. The companies that automate first will have a competitive edge. And those that automate later will struggle, potentially losing more employees than if they had automated earlier.

Automation doesn't have to eliminate the need for human workers. Instead it can free them up to participate in revenue generating activities. There is nothing wrong with data entry, but only a human being can connect meaningfully with another human being in a sales or customer service situation. As machine capacity expands, people are free to do what machines will never be able to do.

Of course most transportation and manufacturing companies use some sort of software already. Some use a simple accounting program, while others might use something more sophisticated that helps them manage invoices and orders as well. But as long as a company is employing people to reconcile bills and match invoices to payments, it is not running as efficiently as possible. Furthermore, it is reducing its scalability and potential for growth, because an increase in the volume of business will automatically lead to a comparable increase in paperwork. Just as it did with One Horn, Stratebo can help grow and scale almost any business while reducing costs.

Better Together

As you might have noticed, what Louis and I do in our individual businesses are really two sides of the same coin. I coach clients to grow and scale their businesses in such a way that frees them up to do what they want. Often a huge part of that is creating systems and automating tasks the way Stratebo Technologies has done for One Horn. I definitely consult Louis whenever a technology or reengineering issue comes up for a client, just as he consults me for marketing and social media strategies for Stratebo.

Both of our businesses involve activities about which Louis and I are individually passionate. Not only are we able to pursue the things we enjoy, but we are also able to diversify our family's sources of income, which only makes sense in an unpredictable world. Although One Horn has started back on its growth trajectory again, from a strategic planning perspective, we would advise any entrepreneur to innovate constantly and keep several irons in the fire. Calculate the likelihood of success of each of your ventures. If the sum of their probabilities is greater than one, you've got to like your chances!

PART TWO

BUILDING BEST PRACTICES

CHAPTER 9

·················

NOW THAT YOU'VE GROWN,
WHO DOES WHAT?

When our entrepreneurial journey began, Cheryl and I worked very long days, grateful just to have basic control of our lives. But ultimately, we wanted more than that. By pivoting first to a brokerage, later to an agent-based brokerage and then refining and automating our systems, we now enjoy the lifestyle we have always wanted. We can travel as often as we like and spend lots of quality time together as a family. We are no longer working late into the night, and we never have to miss a school play or a soccer game.

As you've seen from the previous chapters, we obtained this freedom through a gradual process of ongoing internal innovation. Instead of allowing ourselves to get stuck in an imperfect routine, we constantly evaluated how things were going and what we could improve. This led to regular, detailed analyses of all our systems, which in turn led us to streamline different processes in various ways. If we couldn't automate, we would delegate, outsource, or even hire.

This chapter will offer an overview of how we transformed One Horn from a time-consuming endeavor that required constant attention, to an efficient engine that now runs with very little maintenance from us. Chapter 10, "Automate It!," and Chapter 11, "Outsourcing," will offer more detailed information on automation and outsourcing that can be applied to almost any industry or business.

Continual Learning

Innovation is driven by new ideas. Cheryl's and my commitment to continually exposing ourselves to new ideas has been vital to the ongoing innovation at One Horn. Neither of us viewed our MBAs as the endpoint of our business education, but rather as the launching pad for a lifetime of growth and professional development. The key for us has been taking advantage of top quality business publications and training opportunities, and then immediately discussing what we've learned and how it can help us run our business better.

There are many ways to learn, even when you are not enrolled in a formal educational institution. We both regularly read and discuss business books and articles from publications like the *Economist* and *Harvard Business Review*. We attend Entrepreneurs' Organization (EO) conferences on a regular basis, take notes on all the presentations and debrief afterwards to determine what we can apply to One Horn. The application might involve general principles, or—as in the case of Solange Perret's presentation prompting us to pivot to an agent-based model—specific action steps.

This continual exposure to new ideas and cutting edge innovations from multiple industries has also been vital to our ongoing evaluation of our systems. It is not easy to honestly assess every aspect of the business to determine what is working and what is not. When you have invested a lot of time and effort into a particular strategy or product, it can be very tempting to stick with it regardless of how it is performing.

But sometimes the best decision for your business is to cut an underperforming program or pivot from a strategy that isn't working the way you had planned. As we explained in Chapter 4, "From Surviving to Thriving," we put a lot of effort to get certified as a WBE and an MBE. The certifying bodies encouraged us to pursue lucrative government contracts and large corporations that valued vendor diversity, which seemed like a great idea. But we eventually had to face the fact that those certifications were not producing what we had hoped. The large corporations already had the capacity to handle the brokerage function in house, and the government entities also preferred to work directly with carriers. Neither were worth our time to pursue, so we directed our efforts elsewhere.

Like most entrepreneurs, creative inspiration can hit us at any time, not just when we are reading books or attending seminars. (I have been known to get coding ideas in the middle of the night!) But ultimately, curiosity and a desire to learn are irreplaceable ingredients for anyone who wants to innovate and improve a business. We'll talk more about this kind of strategic thinking in Chapter 13, "Strategic Thinking."

Working Ourselves Out of a Job

Many people have observed that you can buy or start a business and really end up with a job, in the sense that your time is almost as constrained as it would be if you were working for someone else. From the very beginning, our long term plan was to stop working *for* One Horn by getting the company to a point where it could basically run itself. This was the focus of all our innovation and streamlining.

In his 2004 book, *The E-Myth Revisited: Why Most Small Businesses Don't Work and What to do About It,* author Michael Gerber details what business owners need to do to get rid of their job-like duties and create what he calls a "franchise prototype," a business with systems in place that can run well without the owner's constant presence. To do this, Gerber explains, we must be able to fulfill three distinct roles: technician, manager, and entrepreneur. The technician works in the business—making the product or providing the service—while the manager takes care of the logistics of running the company, and the entrepreneur casts the vision and sets the direction for the company. Gerber argues that too many small business owners get caught up in the roles of technician and manager, losing sight of the entrepreneurial big picture in the process.

We worked hard to stay in the entrepreneurial mindset, even while we had to do a lot of work as the technician and manager. One of the ways we did this was by keeping an organizational chart that listed every role that needed to be filled for One Horn to run effectively. We put names beside them (at the time Cheryl's, our former back office employee's, and mine) with the goal of removing Cheryl's and my names from as many tasks as possible.

We regularly examined these tasks and tackled the most time-consuming ones first, with the intention of automating or outsourcing. As you can imagine, it wouldn't make sense for me to spend ten months writing code for a task that would only save an hour a week, so we used a ninety-day guideline. If we could streamline or automate a task by working on it in house for ninety days or less, that's what we would do. If it would take longer than ninety days, we would outsource it or hire someone to take care of it.

The Big Picture

Using this methodical approach, we were gradually able to cross our names off more items on the organizational chart and free up more and more of our time. We then took steps to live the life we wanted. First, we instituted a regular date night each week. Our kids were finally old enough to stay home without a sitter—they even began cooking their own dinners—so we were able to take a little more time for ourselves. We also began to spend more time skiing and doing other things we loved.

Today we travel several weeks out of each year and take more weekends away than we can count. Our business can run no matter where we are (more on this in Chapter 17, "Have Scanner, Will Travel"), and we no longer have to put in full days to ensure smooth, consistent service to our customers. This is what we have always wanted, and we are very grateful.

Occasionally we have been asked if our relatively leisurely lifestyle causes any resentment among our employees or associates. In reality, our drive to become more efficient and continually improve our systems actually helps everyone with whom we work. There is a saying in the transportation industry that agents can never take vacation, because they could lose their entire business in a few days. (Shippers who can't reach an agent at a given moment will just take their business elsewhere.) But our systems have changed that. We have empowered our agents to work remotely if they choose, and have coached anyone who is interested in how to automate and streamline their business the way we have. My constant improvements to the software also save time and effort for everyone concerned.

Business is competitive by nature, but improvement doesn't have to be a zero sum game. You can transform your business in ways that help you, your employees, and your customers. In the next chapters we'll explain how to do just that.

CHAPTER 10

AUTOMATE IT!

AUTOMATE IT!

As you've seen by now, automation was the primary reason that Louis and I were able to grow our business tenfold while actually reducing our workload. Automation has been key to our scalability and vital to our efficiency. And, as you will see in this chapter, this has happened by design, not by accident.

Whenever we are faced with an undertaking that has become repetitive, time-consuming, or just annoying, I have a mantra: "Figure it out without hiring: automate it!" As you know by now, the task of automation typically falls to Louis, because he is the one who writes the code that enables the computer to do the job. But the mantra is still a good one for all business owners to keep in mind.

When Louis worked as a business strategy consultant, he saw firsthand the tendency of companies to become bloated with personnel. When a profitable business is growing, it is very easy for the owner to hire away the tasks he or she doesn't want to do. But often this is just a way of postponing the necessary task of streamlining business processes.

Louis would be brought in as a consultant to assess companies, determine how to make them run more efficiently, and—unfortunately for some people—eliminate positions that were no longer needed. His services were often required because these are very painful changes that can sometimes be almost impossible to accomplish without outside help. He learned from this experience that if you are not taking regular steps to streamline and automate from the very beginning, your company will quickly become weighed down with unnecessary people and inefficient processes.

The Case Against Hiring

While it is sometimes necessary and even desirable to hire, it is important to understand all the reasons why you may want to exhaust all your other options first. Employees cost money in salary and often benefits, if they are working full time. As you become dependent on them to perform certain tasks, their absence or departure can be very costly. And of course there is always the possibility that they may make expensive mistakes or even violate your trust.

While employees have been an important source of innovation in many fields, generally speaking—as we mentioned in the last chapter—they will not innovate themselves out of a job. In other words, if you hire John to do your billing, it is highly unlikely he is going to come to you with an innovation that enables you to do your billing without him!

Furthermore, if you double your volume of business, you will have to double John's hours. If John is already working at capacity, you will have to hire a second employee to help him. Continuing to grow in this way means that you will eventually have to hire a manager. Expand more and you'll need more managers, and then upper level managers to oversee the middle level managers. All this negatively affects your scalability.

Based on these disadvantages, Louis and I developed several questions we would ask ourselves before we hired for a task. Can the task be done more efficiently? Can it be automated or partially automated in under ninety days? Should it be outsourced or partially outsourced? (More on this in the next chapter.)

Naturally there are some functions that cannot be streamlined or automated at all, or not without significant compromise to the quality of the service provided. Customers sometimes want to talk to a live person, and none of us goes to a fine restaurant to be waited on by a robot. Machines can never replace the human touch needed to perform certain functions, and that's as it should be. But you never want to hire people to perform repetitive jobs that don't require any thinking, because such tasks can almost always be done by a machine. The failure to critically examine the alternatives to hiring ends up bloating many businesses and preventing them from being as profitable and scalable as they might be otherwise.

Automation at One Horn

As an agent-based brokerage, One Horn is really a bill-collecting and bill-generating business. How quickly we can process invoices and generate and mail checks determines how long we have to work each day. We have been through several micro-innovations in our billing system, each one saving us more time and effort. As of this writing, we are on the sixth version, which is the most efficient and cost-effective one yet.

When we began, trucking companies would send us paper invoices, which we then had to scan into the system and match to the job number. This was a very time-consuming process, as you might imagine. One of our earliest innovations was getpaid@onehorn.com where we only accepted scanned invoices. This meant the trucking companies scanned the invoices into our system instead of us. This small change not only saved us a great deal of time, but it also enabled the carriers to get their paperwork to us more quickly. This, in turn, helped them get paid faster, so it really was a win for both parties.

After that, Louis programmed the system so it only took a couple of clicks for to match up the invoices with the job numbers. Then he created a barcode system so that scanned invoices were automatically identified and matched with their job numbers as soon as they came in. All that is left for human intervention is verifying that everything is in order.

Although this progressive automation was specific to billing, the procedure can be applied to any business process. First, we thought about each step and determined which ones were repetitive and required no thought. Of those steps, we asked which ones could be eliminated, and which could be done by the computer or a machine. Then we examined which steps could be done more efficiently. Even something as simple as stuffing envelopes—which we will talk about more in the next chapter— can be completed much more quickly if you set up a good system.

Our experience with billing also demonstrates that automation should not be a one-time event. Often when large companies set out to automate, they commission a project with consultants who examine what everyone is doing, and programmers who then write programs to automate those tasks. They typically don't take the time to determine which steps can be eliminated or done more efficiently, and they never come back in a year or two to apply new technological developments to the status quo.

This kind of large scale automation can take several months or even years. When the project is complete, the company has a system that effectively freezes everyone's jobs in place, because it is so expensive to make changes. Essentially, they automate without streamlining. At One Horn, we have automated in smaller increments, tackling one task at a time. This has enabled us to improve our systems as our needs change and technological capabilities increase.

I have also been able to automate portions of my marketing activities (more on these in Chapter 12, "The Marketing Triad: Social Media, Publishing, and Awards"), by using Hootsuite to post on multiple social media platforms at once, and Mail Chimp to send my subscribers links to my biweekly blogs. I learned about these applications at some of the various conferences we attend on a regular basis, as part of the ongoing learning we discussed in the last chapter.

It is important to keep in mind that when we pivoted to the brokerage model, we intentionally automated as much as possible, as well as making our business portable (more on that in Chapter 17, "Have Scanner, Will Travel"). Our desire for flexibility drove these choices, and there were certain opportunities and business models we did not select, because we knew they did not lend themselves to automation.

Not every small business has to be this automation oriented. Families that own convenience stores or restaurants, for example, may truly enjoy interacting with their customers face-to-face on a regular basis, and that's wonderful. However, they can still benefit from having their systems run as smoothly and efficiently as possible. Every business owner can increase profitability and productivity by regularly evaluating their processes and eliminating or automating as many steps as they can.

CHAPTER 11

OUTSOURCING

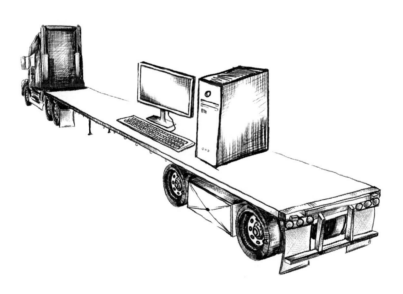

OUTSOURCING

"**S**orry, kids. You were outsourced." You would think that being employed by your parents would offer a little job security, but our children, Alexander and Genevieve, found out otherwise. They had been working—with waning enthusiasm—for One Horn during a phase of our billing process when we still printed our checks at home. Cheryl would sign them by hand and then they had to be placed in envelopes, which needed to be labeled, sealed, stamped, and of course, mailed.

This is the kind of job that doesn't bother you at all when there are just a few envelopes. But when you get to twenty, fifty, or a few hundred, the task becomes unbearably dull. While the children were doing it, we made sure the supplies were laid out in order so they could be as efficient as possible, but as our business grew, it was clear this was not going to be a long-term solution.

We considered automating the task, and at one point we actually purchased a mechanical envelope stuffer off eBay. The giant box arrived, but I never had the courage to open it. Cheryl and I had no problem running the company out of our home, but we were not ready to operate heavy machinery. The inconvenience, cost, and upkeep of the machine turned out to be too much for the volume of paper we generated, even as we grew.

Finally, we learned of a company in Connecticut that could receive our electronic checks, then label, stuff, seal, stamp, and mail our envelopes for less money than it took for us to do it ourselves. Suddenly, the decision was a no-brainer, and Alexander and Genevieve were out of a job!

Optimizing Productivity

Most of us are told growing up that if we work hard enough, we will be successful. This is good advice as far as it goes, but hard work by itself doesn't guarantee productivity, let alone success. I have a friend who used to say that an elevator works hard all day, but it still ends up in the same place it started. Kind of harsh, but sadly true.

As a Gazelles Coach, Cheryl teaches her clients the execution principles from Verne Harnish's *Scaling Up*. This involves selecting and documenting a few key priorities that will move a company forward, and then identifying the goals they should be setting in their individual roles to support the company's priorities. By adding specific, measurable, achievable, realistic, and time-bound (SMART) key performance indicators (KPIs) to their goals, employees can now see whether the tasks they have been performing on a given day or week are productive, or just busy work.

We mentioned in the last chapter that streamlining is a vital part of any solution, whether it's automation or outsourcing. One of the greatest advantages of not having a surplus of human labor around is that you don't just delegate a task away without reducing it to the absolute minimum number of steps or minutes required to complete it. Once you've streamlined a task, it will be much easier and cheaper to outsource what remains than it would have been if you had skipped that step.

Envelope stuffing didn't lend itself to automation for One Horn, but automation was still part of the solution. The company in Connecticut would not have been able to save us much time if we had had to generate each file individually before we sent it to them. Our success was due to all the automation we explained in the last chapter, combined with the outsourcing that provided the best overall solution to our billing needs.

This kind of partial outsourcing can work in a lot of different ways. Although we developed all of Stratebo in house, we did buy several pieces of code from outside vendors that we merged into our system. For example, it would have taken me a year or so to write a PDF-handling code to deal with all the check images. That violated my ninety day rule, so we bought it from an outside vendor.

Buying code can sometimes be problematic, because most vendors will try to charge you by the number of users that you have. This, as you know by now, will make your business less scalable. Fortunately, some vendors do permit you to buy the code outright, which has enabled us to expand our number of users without increasing costs.

To make the most of outsourcing, you must take the time to understand your process thoroughly before you try to hand it off to someone else. When we outsourced our envelopes, we were sure to anticipate that checks sent to Canada would need extra postage. We created a system that automatically generated a note for the company alerting them to the presence of an international address and reminding them to apply sufficient postage.

We could have easily told ourselves that this wouldn't happen very often and not worried about it. But this would have meant dealing with phone calls and questions down the road. Take the time to document and explain everything you need done before you outsource, anticipating as many potential issues as possible. This effort on the front end will save you time and money in the long run.

Outsourcing Your Weaknesses

All of us have strengths and weaknesses as individuals, and these will often be reflected in our businesses. It frequently makes sense to outsource the aspects of the business that you don't do as well, especially if they cannot be automated. Even large corporations will acquire other companies to give them capabilities they don't already have.

In fact, you could look at two of the major pivots we made with One Horn—from a trucking company to a brokerage and from a brokerage to an agent-based brokerage—as outsourcing the aspects of transportation that were not our strengths. The first pivot outsourced the truck ownership and maintenance to the trucking companies. The second outsourced the sales and dispatching to the agents. Truck maintenance, sales and dispatching must be done by people, not machines, so it made sense to cooperate with individuals who wanted to do those tasks more than we did.

More recently, we hired a door-opening company to help us with our corporate agent model. We know that we can close a high percentage of our sales once we get in front of the right people. But neither Cheryl nor I relish the thought of doing hundreds of cold calls to get in the door. The company we have engaged specializes in this step in the sales process and does it very well.

When It Makes Sense to Hire

Sometimes it makes more sense to hire someone than it does to outsource a task. We have kept a single back office employee for most of One Horn's existence. Unfortunately, she left us unexpectedly, so before we hired a replacement we conducted a time and effort analysis on what she used to do. We came to the harsh realization that we had gradually automated many of her functions. We have only recently hired someone part time to do some of her former duties.

When you do hire, you want to keep everyone working at capacity. It is usually best to keep a careful chart of the hours everyone is working to ensure that you are optimizing your productivity. And if you find that your employee or employees don't have enough to do, it's time to grow the company again!

Just as you need to evaluate people carefully before you hire them, you need to do the same with any company that you decide to work with. But even with due diligence, outsourcing doesn't always work out the way you want. Once, Cheryl and I decided to outsource some of our programming to another company in order to finish a particular project. Unfortunately, the company—though eager—turned out not to possess the skills necessary to do what we needed. After they missed a couple of deadlines, we decided it was time to walk away.

Ultimately, you should outsource or hire if you don't have the resources, drive, or desire to so something that you need done, or when someone else can do it more efficiently or less expensively than you. Obviously, the company in Connecticut that handles our envelopes can do it more cheaply because our job is just a tiny percentage of their overall volume.

For those of us who put our hearts and souls into our businesses, it can be hard to give up certain tasks. And the reality is that the people you hand these tasks to—whether they are your employees or the employees of another company—will probably not do them exactly the way you would. But that doesn't mean they will not do a good job, nor that it isn't time to let the task go. At the end of the day, outsourcing really enables you to spend your time doing what you do best, which is part of building the life you want.

CHAPTER 12

. . . .

THE MARKETING TRIAD: SOCIAL MEDIA, PUBLISHING, AND AWARDS

How can you market your small business with the savvy of a large corporation but without a huge marketing budget? Both Louis and I came from multinational companies, and we knew we were looking for big-company talent for One Horn. So we set out to show the world that One Horn was so much more than just a home-based startup, and we did it without spending a fortune.

Drawing on my corporate experience, an Entrepreneurs' Organization (EO) event with Gary Vaynerchuk of the Wine Library and author of *Crush It: Why Now is the Time to Cash in on Your Passion,* and additional research, I developed a three-pronged strategy for marketing our company on a tiny budget: social media, publishing, and awards. By claiming the transportation footprint in social media, publishing a content-rich blog with solutions for our target market, and winning industry awards that generated third party media coverage, I knew we could go a long way toward persuading the best freight agents to give One Horn a try.

The first steps in the standard corporate marketing procedure are to articulate reasons for the target audience to buy what you are selling and craft a message tailored around those reasons. Then you determine what kind of media your target audience is consuming, then purchase time or ad space in the right media. I followed this same procedure for One Horn, utilizing a neuromarketing strategy to craft my message with language centered on the "pain points" of freight agents.

In their book *Neuromarketing: Understanding the Buy*

Buttons in Your Customer's Brain, authors Patrick Renoise and Christophe Morin explain that pain is the difference between a desired state and an existing state. They write, "To properly diagnose a prospect's pain, you simply need to answer the following four questions: 1. What is the source of the prospect's most prominent pain? 2. What level or degree is the intensity of that pain? 3. What is the level of urgency requiring the pain to be solved? 4. Is my prospect aware of and does he/she acknowledge his/her own pain?"

So, instead of talking about ourselves, we spoke compellingly about the pain freight agents experienced: brokers who didn't pay carriers on time, cumbersome technology, and getting lost in the crowd at a large brokerage that didn't care about them. We then focused our marketing message on how working for One Horn would make freight agents' lives easier.

If I had been at my old corporate job, I would have then purchased television, radio, or print ads, depending on the target consumer. For example, if I were trying to reach stay-at-home moms, I might purchase ads on daytime television talk shows or soap operas. If I were reaching men between the ages of 18 and 44, I would probably purchase ad time on sports or news radio programs.

But these forms of advertising are very expensive, and they would not have suited One Horn's purposes, as our target audience was not part of the general population reached by mass media advertising. We were targeting an estimated eight to ten thousand freight agents nationwide, about two thousand of whom were open to move. Obviously, this is quite difficult. To add to our challenges, neither Louis nor I had grown up in the industry as many agents had. We found ourselves outsiders in a community where trucking often stretched back for generations.

We overcame these difficulties by online advertising on industry websites, and the previously mentioned triad of social media, publishing, and awards. This strategy not only cost very little money, but it also enabled us to become thought leaders and problem solvers in the trucking industry, ultimately increasing our business tenfold.

Social Media

Most of us have heard the basics of sales on a tight budget: develop your elevator pitch, attend networking events, ask satisfied clients for referrals and so on. While I am a very social person and enjoy networking events a great deal, they are not generally industry-specific. Although such gatherings might have been useful when we were looking for shippers, the chances that I would bump into a freight agent who was open to switching brokerages at a local Chamber of Commerce event were slim to none.

In his book *Crush It,* Gary Vaynerchuk explained how the social media revolution was changing the way business was done. After hearing him speak in 2010, we decided to claim the social media footprint in trucking and transportation. The timing was perfect, because larger transportation companies were still dismissing it as a passing fad. Furthermore, we were convinced that investing in social media could enable us to have a very large impact for very little money.

It's easy to think of trucking as a largely offline activity. After all, the internet doesn't drive all those loads of freight across the country. But all those invoices and dispatch orders that were once done on white boards and carbon paper (now I'm really dating myself!) are now done entirely online. Agents spend most of their days on the phone and in front of their computers, booking freight and talking to drivers and customers. Occasionally they will visit customers in person, but in general social media is an ideal way for them to communicate with the outside world.

To reach our target market, we first had to determine which social media platform agents were using and then build a digital environment for them to visit once they heard our message. In our case, the social media platform was LinkedIn and the digital environment was the mini-website I mentioned in Chapter Five, "Building the Freight Agent Model." This was targeted specifically at agents, explaining our freight agent program and what an innovative company we were. It was separate from our main One Horn site, which still targeted shippers.

Once we had the website ready, I joined several industry groups on LinkedIn and regularly hosted discussions on the trucking and transportation issues that were hot at the time. I also started participating in other people's LinkedIn conversations about various topics. This enabled me to engage business colleagues all over the country and really start getting our name out to the right people.

This kind of networking, along with online advertising on industry websites, ended up being far more effective than much pricier forms of marketing. We also developed strong connections with other industry leaders, including some competitors. I even got very helpful advice from another broker about some of my messaging, a sign that we were making our way from "outsiders" to becoming a part of the trucking community.

Of course, now larger corporations have caught on and hired directors of social media who spend all day working to penetrate and dominate these digital spaces. The digital marketspace is much more competitive and unclaimed turf is much harder to find. But the principle of discovering where your target or core consumer "hangs out" online still holds. Retail customers might be found more frequently on Facebook, while Business to Business (B2B) customers are still probably on LinkedIn. Twitter can be used in conjunction with other platforms to link to Facebook posts, blog posts, or LinkedIn conversations. Even Instagram and Pinterest can be used for products and services that are more visual, while Snapchat can serve those targeting younger audiences. When marketing on social media, remember to emphasize what Bob Bloom calls your *uncommon offering*: what you can do for your customers that no one else can do.

Publishing

One day I was flipping through an issue of *IT Magazine*, published by Internet Truckstop, a "load board" that connects truckers with loads they can haul. There I saw my picture at the bottom of an article. I glanced over the text and realized that I had indeed written those words, yet I knew I had never submitted my piece to this publication. After getting over my initial surprise, I realized that the magazine had simply reprinted one of my blogs, which were publicly available. Naturally, I got in touch with them, and Louis and I became regular contributors.

I began my bi-weekly blog for freight agents as a way to share helpful content, establish Louis and me as thought leaders in the industry, and attract agents who would be good fits for One Horn. My posts covered a variety of topics, from improving operational efficiency and personal effectiveness to hints for finding new customers and increasing profitability. All these posts were designed to help freight agents improve their businesses and their personal lives.

Regularly publishing helpful content is vital to developing a following, so instead of dealing with a deadline every other week, I wrote six months' worth of blog posts in just a few weeks. To develop the content, I came up with a list of possible topics drawn from my regular reading and seminar training. Then I ran it by Louis and other colleagues for feedback. Once I had refined my list, I simply blocked off a few hours each day to write my posts until they were all done. This enabled me to publish them on schedule without any pressure.

Louis has also published regularly, particularly on the intersection of technology and transportation. His articles are usually longer than my blog entries, and appear in about half the issues of *IT Magazine*. His writing typically focuses on agents' and truckers' technology needs and concerns. He has covered a variety of relevant topics from how to evade computer viruses, to how to avoid purchasing obsolete software.

All of these efforts have helped us establish our credibility, improve our search engine optimization (SEO), and enabled agents to learn about us as a fast-growing company with top-of-the line technology. This went a long way toward convincing agents to work with One Horn.

Awards

After attending a presentation by fellow entrepreneur and friend, Matt Shoup, I learned that applying for industry and business awards is a great way to generate positive public relations exposure at little to no cost to your company. The difference between advertising and public relations is that the first is a paid message that you control, while the second is reported by a third party. The latter is free and often carries a greater level of credibility—because it's not you talking about your own company—but it's also mostly out of your hands.

I investigated and applied for awards for which One Horn was eligible, focusing on our growth trajectory and the fact that we are a woman-owned business. Each time we won, I would send out a press release to relevant publications. It paid off: from 2012 to 2015, One Horn was ranked among the fifty fastest-growing women-owned/led businesses in North America by the Women Presidents' Organization and American Express.

I also applied for NJBIZ's "New Jersey's Fastest Growing Companies" ranking, and we were ranked two years in a row in 2013 and 2014. I earned a spot among the "50 Best Women in Business," an award sponsored by NJBIZ and a Brava Award from Smart CEO Magazine in 2014. I was also named among the Top 25 Leading Women Entrepreneurs in New Jersey in

2015, and subsequently served on their advisory board.

These awards generated great articles about One Horn in industry publications and in some of our large regional newspapers. Industry associations would print our press releases in their newsletters and sometimes the local paper would send a photographer to capture images for a feature article. This kind of third party publicity really helped our SEO and established us an authority in trucking and transportation.

We were able to leverage all these awards toward recognition on social media. People I had never met would congratulate us on LinkedIn, and when candidates searched for us on the internet, they would find lots of favorable articles. There was virtually no downside, since we generated only positive publicity and were able to handle the increased volume of business without any major issues.

Of course, social media and the rest of the internet are constantly changing, so to market effectively you have to be ready to adapt as well. Our online advertising in certain media outlets is no longer as effective as it used to be, largely because of changes in the transportation industry that we've already mentioned. And just like kids have abandoned Facebook for Snapchat (as of this writing), professionals may gravitate to some other platform, causing us to pivot as well. Regardless of these changes, social media, publishing, and awards remain a highly effective way to market your small business at minimal cost.

CHAPTER 13

· · · · · · · · · · · · · · · ·

STRATEGIC THINKING

Just before Louis and I became entrepreneurs, I made a choice that would
have a profound effect on One Horn's
future: I said "no" to diamond earrings.

Many of my friends at the time had lovely
diamond earrings, and Louis—being the wonderful husband he
is—asked me if I wanted some too. Being the practical woman
I am, I thought about it, and told him that I would rather finish
our basement, build a deck, and put in a hot tub, all of which we
could do comfortably for the cost of the earrings in question.
And, as you know by now, that hot tub became our "think tank"
where the future of One Horn was discussed and shaped.

Making the Time

It's extremely easy to neglect strategic thinking when your
business demands so much of your time and energy just to
keep things going, but the hot tub made it something to look
forward to. Some nights we would just decompress from a week
of work, going over what went well and what we could improve.
On others we would gather with a few friends (with wine and
hors d'oeuvres, of course!) and present our ideas to get their
feedback.

Too often, small business owners do all their strategic
planning on the fly, instead of setting aside sufficient time to
contemplate the short and long term options before them. In a
large corporation, you are not only expected to develop a plan
for the future of your department, but you also have to present
evidence that justifies why you think your plan will work. Both

Louis and I found this to be a very useful exercise as entrepreneurs, although we opted for bathing suits instead of business suits.

Trying to convince our business savvy colleagues that a particular plan made sense forced us to think through our decisions much more thoroughly than we would have otherwise. For example, before we pivoted from a trucking company to a brokerage, as we discussed in Chapter 3, "A Tale of Two Companies," Louis put together a PowerPoint presentation with all the relevant numbers related to the earnings and expenditures of One Horn Trucking (the trucking company) and One Horn Transportation (the brokerage). Once we had everything written down, the right decision became clear, even if it was still painful.

Our hot tub has also been a tremendous source of creative and inspired ideas. As author Barbara Frederickson explains, "Positivity opens us. The first core truth about positive emotions is that they open our hearts and our minds, making us more receptive and more creative." So whether or not you invest in a hot tub like we did, be sure to make time for the activities that put you in a positive frame of mind.

Calculating Risk

Strategic planning often boils down to weighing risk against reward. Of course, we had borrowed a great deal of money to buy One Horn, so we really didn't have a choice but to succeed. Some people respond to this kind of situation by making impulsive or unwise choices, but we knew we needed to weigh all our steps carefully without failing to act (more on this in the next chapter!).

Assessing risk is a completely different process in a small business than it is in a large corporation. Rather than taking the chance of being awarded a smaller budget next time, you are really gambling with your own money. It's also important to remember that only a very small percentage of new ideas actually work, so strategic thinking is in many ways a volume game. Often the best way forward is to come up with enough ideas you can try at minimal risk, and have an acceptable way to evaluate how well they are working. Then you can adjust and try again.

You also don't want to let yourself get so emotionally attached to one particular idea that you are unwilling to cut it if it's not working out. For example, we tried LinkedIn banner advertising on the advice of a colleague. The risk was relatively low because it was pay-per-click, so we would only be charged in proportion to how much interest the ads were actually generating. That said, it really didn't bring us any meaningful leads, so we discontinued it. You have to be willing to try and give up on new things in order to make progress.

Feedback and Advice

One of the aspects of working in corporate America that I really did miss as an entrepreneur was conversing regularly with colleagues who could offer feedback on my ideas and advice for my decisions. This kind of interaction is important not only for encouragement, but also for the valuable exchange of ideas, and the opportunity to benefit from the variety of experiences and perspectives that different people bring to the table.

In addition to our hot tub advisors—many of whom had corporate backgrounds—Louis and I were able to connect with several entrepreneurial groups. Because these were fellow business owners, we shared many of the same struggles and challenges. These groups became an additional circle of advisors for us, while enabling us to contribute to the development of other companies as well.

I joined the Wharton Club of New Jersey's Entrepreneurs' Circle, a group of about six Wharton alumni who owned businesses and met monthly. A couple of other groups I belonged to—the local chapters of the Commerce and Industry Association and the Women Presidents' Organization—had closer to eighteen members. Later Louis and I joined the Entrepreneurs Organization, which hosted many valuable conferences we have already mentioned. All our meetings were confidential and a great source of wisdom and encouragement.

Most of these organizations require a minimum of one million in annual sales for the owner to join, so they don't work for everyone. If you do not own a business, you can check out the Young Presidents' Organization, Vistage, and similar groups. You could also consider starting your own mastermind group among business owners in a particular locale.

Other Resources

As we've already mentioned, Louis and I read business books on a regular basis. Both of our MBA programs focused on strategic thinking within a corporate context, but many of the books we have found helpful provided insight into strategic thinking for small and medium-sized businesses.

Some of these books are very well known, such as *Think and Grow Rich* by Napoleon Hill and *The E-Myth Revisited* by Michael Gerber, which we mentioned in Chapter 9, "Now that You've Grown, Who Does What?" While doing sales for One Horn, I also benefited from several sales books by Dale Carnegie and Jeffrey Gitomer.

We learned a great deal from *The Four-Hour Workweek* by Tim Ferriss. Although the premise of a four-hour workweek sounds farfetched at first, we really did glean some useful principles from it, including our commitment to make One Horn mobile (which we'll talk more about in Chapter 17, "Have Scanner, Will Travel"). We would encourage every business owner to read it with an open mind.

As we scaled our business and attended an Entrepreneurs' Organization four-day seminar at MIT for key executives of member businesses, we learned more about *Mastering The Rockefeller Habits* directly from Verne Harnish, also author of *Scaling Up*, the basis of the teachings I use in my Gazelles coaching practice. In addition to discussing our business model with Verne, we also had the opportunity to review its efficiency with Greg Crabtree, author of *Simple Numbers, Straight Talk, Big Profits!*, one of the key contributors to the Cash module of *Scaling Up*.

The Lean Startup by Eric Ries taught us the principle of the minimum viable product and how to innovate continuously, instead of betting the farm on the first iteration of a product or service. Ries's book turns the intricately crafted five-year business plan on its head and instead advocates a more general "business model canvass." In his model, you take your minimum product or service to market, and start getting feedback from actual customers, adding features gradually in response.

Lastly, we benefited a great deal from *Exponential Organizations: Why new organizations are ten times better, faster, and cheaper than yours (and what to do about it)* by Salim Ismail. All these books helped us toward our endgame with One Horn, which was to be a flexible, scalable, portable company that could run with very little input from us. Whatever your long-term goals are for your business, there is a plethora of information available to make them happen.

CHAPTER 14

·······················

ACT, ACT, ACT

As you know by now, both Cheryl and I love to learn, and we take advantage of as many opportunities as we can for training and exposure to new ideas. But you can attend dozens of seminars, participate in monthly entrepreneurial gatherings, and read hundreds of books without really affecting your business in a meaningful way. You can even go through all the strategic planning exercises we covered in the last chapter without making much actual progress. Knowledge and planning only become powerful when you put them into action.

Of course, some entrepreneurs act too impulsively, failing to think through the implications of their decisions. But many others fail to act at all, accumulating knowledge and ideas without ever doing anything with them. This chapter will teach you how to act on what you learn in a way that is both productive and practical.

Converting Knowledge into Action

Productive action doesn't always end in "success" in the sense that you get exactly the results you are hoping for. As we've already discussed, most new ideas will not work out. However, the right kinds of action will always teach you something valuable about what you do and how you do it.

One of the keys to translating any newly obtained knowledge into productive action is to analyze it as soon as possible as we have also demonstrated in our "Triple-A Method." If you wait too long, the information will not be fresh in your mind, and you may lose many of the valuable applications to your business. Cheryl and I often compare notes right after a conference or seminar. Because we tend to approach problems differently, we often walk away from the same session with very different ideas.

We review what we each learned and then assess the possible action steps we could take for our company in response to the new information. We weigh the risks involved with each step and evaluate if and how they fit into our overall business plan. We then classify those potential actions into three main categories:

The No Brainers

These are the simple, often low-risk actions that are easy for us to take right now. For example, Cheryl and I heard a speaker who explained in great detail the cost of acquiring a new customer. He elaborated on the resources required to locate, connect with, and sign a new client in any business, and then he asked why companies don't offer larger incentives for referrals.

Cheryl and I discussed what the speaker said and agreed right then and there to increase the incentive five-fold for our agents who brought a new agent on board. Right away, we had two agents begin working deliberately to persuade some of their former colleagues to switch to our brokerage, all because it was now much more worth their time to try. One was very successful, enabling us to sign several high-powered agents with strong earning potential. We are happy to pay the extra incentive, because in the long run it will benefit us tremendously.

This action didn't require extensive planning or research, and was easy to implement. There was little risk involved, since we wouldn't pay any money unless a new agent actually signed. If it hadn't worked for some reason, we could have easily reversed the decision. All these factors made the decision a no brainer.

Naturally, not every no brainer works out. LinkedIn banner advertising works for lots of businesses, but it didn't work for ours. Still, you'll never know which ideas will work until you try at least some of them.

The Down-the-Roads

Some action steps are very good ideas, but require careful planning before implementation. When we came up with our corporate agent model of business, we knew it was a powerful and potentially disruptive idea. We knew we had to move on it. But we later discovered it would need more work and refinement before it could truly disrupt the marketplace.

Some actions might be good for your company eventually, but the timing isn't right yet. We had a terrific suggestion for an innovation in our software, but it won't make sense to work on it until other facets of our business have grown, and we have more users. These are the ideas you put in the slow cooker for a while and take out when they're ready.

Some actions involve a great deal of risk or upfront investment, and so they should be researched carefully before they are taken. This is a perfect time to confer with a mastermind group or entrepreneurial advisors like those we mentioned in the last chapter. These kinds of steps require a lot of patient investigation in order to determine if and when they are the right thing to do.

The Discards

Alas, not every great idea is right for every organization. And some of the potential action steps Cheryl and I come up with simply don't apply to our industry or fit well with our plan for our company. This does not mean they are a total loss. Chances are they may benefit a client in Cheryl's business coaching practice, or some of our colleagues with different kinds of companies or goals.

It is still a useful exercise to translate your information into possible action steps, even if you do not end up taking them. Remember, we are not counting on one single action as a surfire way to double our business. They are just ideas that we can try. If they work, we continue them, adjusting and improving as we go. If they don't work, we simply stop and try something else.

Setting up Experiments

When you understand that the market and the economy as a whole are constantly changing, you will recognize your need for constant innovation. This means that instead of waiting for an outside event to make your current business model, product or service obsolete, you are always working to improve what you what you do and how you do it.

All of us learned the scientific method in school: you formulate a hypothesis—an educated guess about the way you think something will work—and you develop a procedure to test it. Then you run your experiment, measuring the various factors you want to observe. Based on the results, you draw conclusions about whether or not your hypothesis was correct. This is the same basic method we apply when we try new ideas for our business.

The marketplace is full of unpredictable and unmeasurable factors that prevent us from being able to run and repeat business experiments with scientific precision. But we should still try to learn as much as we can by trying new ideas with the intention of systematically observing what happens. Looking at your actions as experiments also helps you avoid putting too much hope in the results of any one decision. And ultimately, experience will provide you with wisdom and understanding that no book or seminar can supply.

Small-scale experimentation can be especially helpful if you are contemplating a large change that will significantly affect your revenue, your employees, or your customers. A chef would never serve a new recipe to a guest unless he or she had tasted it first, and we never put computer code into production until it's been tested. Long before we got out of trucking and became solely a brokerage, we had experimented with running a brokerage on the side.

Depending on your industry or the nature of your company, you may not want to run too many experiments at once. You also want to be sure that you give your new ideas enough time to show whether or not they work. In addition, you must be willing to abandon something when the experiment suggests it will not work on a larger scale.

Developing an Exit Strategy

Even if you do not intend to sell your business any time soon, it is very wise to begin developing an exit strategy and take action to put it into place. This forces you to think about any issues that would prevent someone else from wanting to purchase it. When Cheryl and I started thinking this way, we discovered a few aspects of One Horn that made sense to adjust anyway.

Developing an exit strategy is a bit like preparing to put your house on the market. You could wait to replace the carpet, and paint and upgrade the kitchen and bathrooms until you are ready to move out. Or you could take care of some of those things now and have a chance to enjoy them before you hand the home to someone else.

Some things to consider when preparing your exit strategy are any unresolved legal issues, how your cash flow is looking on paper, and the state of your business's image within your target market. You should also think about your assets and your systems, and how desirable these will appear to a new owner.

Strategic buyers—buyers who are willing to pay more for your company than it's currently worth because you have some kind of "secret sauce" they can leverage in their own business— are really paying for future value. This is much better than selling to someone who is buying for the future value of your current revenue stream. If a buyer views your presence as part of that future value, you might get stuck working until you are no longer needed. Many entrepreneurs don't get to sell their businesses and ride off into the sunset with a pile of cash. Most buyers want sellers to accept earn-outs and stay on working as an employee or consultant for a period of time. If you can put a management team in place in advance so you are not needed, you may be able to avoid this when you sell. We have a friend who actually physically moved his office to another location for a period of time prior to the sale of his business to prove that his management team could run without him.

Thinking about an exit strategy led us to develop Stratebo as a cloud/subscription-based Software as a Service (SaaS), instead of just as a Windows-based application. This had the short-term effect of making the software a potential revenue stream on its own, as well as making the company more appealing to potential buyers in the long run.

Taking action to implement what you have learned, or to experiment with new ideas, can be a little scary. Every action involves risk, but not taking action involves risk as well. If we do not work to improve our companies on a regular basis, we risk becoming obsolete while the rest of the world changes around us. So don't wait too long. Put something from this chapter into action soon!

CHAPTER 15

....

TREASURY MANAGEMENT: HOW WE MANAGE CASH FLOW...DAILY

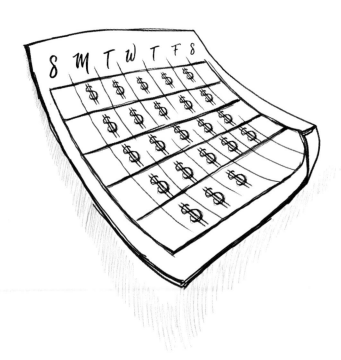

Working as a brand manager in corporate America, I never thought about the company's cash flow. I thought about money, because I was responsible for my profit and loss (P&L) statement. I had to forecast how many units of a product we would sell and keep our production costs at a reasonable level. I also had to stay within the marketing budget, which we calculated as a percentage of sales. But cash flow was never on my mind.

After Louis and I bought One Horn, however, we quickly learned the truth of the old maxim, "Revenue is vanity, profit is sanity, cash is king." I became obsessed with cash. How much did we have in the bank? How much was coming in the mail today? And when were those vendors going to cash the checks I just mailed to them? It took a while, but we finally learned to manage cash flow effectively with a minimum of time, energy, and stress.

Mind the Gap

As we discussed in earlier chapters, late-paying shippers made us revenue positive, but cash flow negative. We couldn't bill our shippers until we received the carrier invoice, but we had to pay our carriers within thirty days or risk losing them as suppliers. Some carriers needed their money even faster, which we would offer them for a 5-percent discount.

All this meant we had to bill our shippers as soon as we received the carrier invoice, and hope they paid on time. Even if everything went smoothly, there was likely to be a gap of a few days between the time we cut the check for the carrier and received payment from the shipper. Without substantial cash reserves, this can be a huge problem in the trucking industry, where hundreds of thousands of dollars change hands in a day.

We had no intention of being late on our bills just because people were late paying us. In fact, we have never intentionally paid late in the entire history of our company. Occasionally, there have been errors that caused a delay. (We are down to a couple per year.) These were almost always due to a carrier's failure to update its address, which caused the check to be sent to the wrong location. Now we even had an automatic email that alerts vendors to the address we have on file, and enables them to change it easily if necessary.

But our commitment to pay on time left the problem of sufficient funds in the bank to cover those payments. Eventually, we addressed this gap with a low interest line of credit, which we'll explain in detail in the next chapter. But even with this in place, we needed to shorten the payment cycle to avoid borrowing any more than was absolutely necessary.

Getting Paid

No one goes to an Ivy League school with dreams of working in accounts receivable. But a few months after we bought One Horn, there I was, calling companies that owed us money and trying to shame them into paying their bills. I even drove to the New Jersey-Pennsylvania state line once to pick up a check from a particularly delinquent company. It was a rude awakening to say the least.

TREASURY MANAGEMENT

As a general principle, I was taught to pay my bills on time, so it really never occurred to me that other people wouldn't think the same way. I was shocked to discover that some very large companies with good reputations didn't seem to care when they paid their bills. The fact that we had signed a contract in which they agreed to pay us at a certain time did not seem to faze them in the least.

The most urgent step in addressing our cash flow issue was doing everything possible to get our shippers to pay us promptly. First, we had to learn that paying "on time" means different things to different customers. Some companies state that they pay in fifteen days, but the fifteen days doesn't begin until someone signs off on the invoice, rather than the date the invoice is actually received.

Furthermore, some companies (and some government entities) pay in sixty, ninety, or even one hundred twenty days as a matter of policy. They essentially manage their cash flow issues by forcing their vendors to wait for their money. (Louis has pointed out that this practice unnecessarily inflates their shipping costs since oftentimes vendors must borrow to cover the gap, but no one ever listens!) Although some of these jobs were lucrative in terms of volume, we made the decision not to work with any customers who didn't commit to pay within thirty days. Borrowing money to float their loads for two or three months cut into our profit margins too much to make the jobs worthwhile.

Second, I learned that I had to make One Horn our shippers' top-of-mind creditor. They likely owed money to multiple vendors, so we needed to make sure that we were first on the list to get paid. In the beginning, this meant making reminder phone calls and emailing invoices multiple times. But to do this for each shipper would be a full -time job, especially as our business grew. So Louis and I did what you would expect us to do: we automated the collections process.

Now with the click of a mouse, we can email a company a complete summary of its open invoices with us. If payment has not been received within twenty days of the initial invoice, the system automatically generates a customized email that provides all the information necessary and attaches a current statement. Then it offers the option to add a personalized note if we need to. Although the system still requires a person to double check all the information, I can easily send a hundred customers their statements in 10 minutes. This helps keep us top-of-mind and goes a long way toward shortening the payment cycle.

Even after we automated the collections process, I would still make phone calls to chronically late customers. But I did so as the president of One Horn, not the clerk of accounts receivable. I would ask to speak to the president of the company that owed us money, in order to make that person feel embarrassed enough to pay us. On a couple of occasions, I had to involve outside organizations to help persuade companies to pay. Whenever collection becomes that much trouble, we will terminate the professional relationship with the company in question after we have received final payment.

Watching the Numbers

We all know we have to reconcile our books at the end of the year to pay our taxes, and for a long time best practices dictated that businesses (and households) should reconcile accounts monthly to avoid a nightmare in December or January. But this norm was established before we had online banking and did hundreds if not thousands of transactions in a single month.

As soon as One Horn started to grow, Louis and I made the decision to reconcile the books daily. Fortunately, QuickBooks or similar programs make reconciling easy. While it could be tempting to avoid thinking about the balance in our business account, particularly when money was tight, this was the only responsible way we could run our brokerage.

We also ran reports twice a week so we could determine when each of our client companies cut their checks. Once we were aware of these patterns, we could make much more accurate predictions for how much money would be in our account on any given day. Watching these numbers closely enabled us to borrow as little as possible, minimizing what we paid in interest.

Keeping a close eye on your balances and reconciling your accounts each day will make your end of the year accounting a piece of cake. It's much easier to remember the details of a certain transaction the day it goes through instead of weeks later. And you will make much better decisions when you know how much money you actually have at any given time.

A business friend of mine once told me, "Customers are only customers if they pay you. You are not a bank." When you are struggling to keep your business afloat, it can seem like a good idea to hang on to chronically late-paying customers who keep promising to pay. But this often forces you to borrow money to cover what they owe.

Although easier said than done, we have made it a point not to do business with customers who treat us like their bank. It is always painful to give up potential revenue, but in the long run this policy has saved us untold stress and headaches. Ultimately, the best thing you can do with late or non-paying customers is to fire them.

CHAPTER 16

MANAGING BUSINESS CREDIT

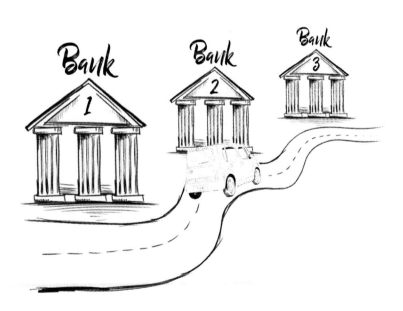

We often run our businesses like we run our own households. If you live modestly, you probably aren't going to worry about renting premium office space on the trendiest boulevard downtown. On the other hand if you like luxury cars and designer clothing, you might want to outfit your business in similar style.

Fortunately Cheryl and I share the same financial values. We do not spend extravagantly, and we live well below our means. We have also done our best to run One Horn the same way. We work out of our home, we have no fulltime employees, and we only take a salary for ourselves when we are profitable. Furthermore, we have used increased profits to pay off our business debt. But this doesn't mean we are debt free.

Good Debt, Bad Debt

Growing up, most of us learned that it is okay to borrow money for a house, as long as the monthly payment is affordable. After all, you need somewhere to live, you can write off the interest on the mortgage, and the house will generally increase in value over time. On the other hand, it's a bad idea to use credit cards to purchase furniture, clothing, vacations, or other consumable non-necessities (unless you pay them off every month), because you could end up paying several times their value in interest.

In the same way, not all business debt is the same. There is bad business debt: debt at high interest rates or incurred for items that are not directly related to revenue generation. We learned the hard way when we bought One Horn that business-to-business loans are not subject to usury laws, which means that interest rates can be 45 percent or even higher. (When we discovered this, we renegotiated these loans and retired them as quickly as possible.)

There are also factoring companies that buy your receivable invoices at a discount. That service is almost like payday advance loans for small businesses. These companies charge up to 5 percent on every bill, but if the bill is not paid in thirty days, they often take all the money back. Factoring does work in many circumstances, but you have to make sure that your business generates margins much higher than the fees the factoring companies charge.

And then there is business debt that is not so bad. We were able to get a line of credit from a bank at a much lower rate of interest than we could get on a personal credit card. We could dip into it when we needed it, and pay it back as the checks came in. It was "good" debt, because our need for it was a consequence of doing a larger volume of business.

A huge corporation might have been able to do this with cash reserves of its own. But as we've already mentioned, trucking and transportation transactions involve hundreds of thousands of dollars. The more our business expanded, the larger the potential cash flow gap when some checks came a few days late. Like most small businesses, we were simply not able to keep millions in reserve at any one time. The credit line from the bank wasn't a fund we used to buy office furniture or new computers. It was a tool to help us serve our agents better and expand our business.

The Mini-Roadshow

"Well if I'd known I was competing to give you this loan, I'd have given you a better rate!"

The bank representative slammed down the phone in Cheryl's ear, and she looked at me in disbelief. The man was indignant that we had not gone with the credit line he offered us, choosing instead one of the two other competitive bids we had received. After we had recovered from the shock of his total lack of professionalism, we both had to laugh. Who would have thought we would have banks competing over the opportunity to lend us money!

Having a strong relationship with your bank can be incredibly helpful. For example, they may choose not to bounce your check even if you do not have sufficient funds in your account, because they trust you will settle the balance promptly. They may also choose to clear certain checks you deposit more quickly, because they know that those checks come from large or reliable companies. But this kind of relationship is hard to develop your first year in business, before you have a proven track record.

When we first approached a local bank for a line of credit, all it wanted to know was how much our house was worth, how much was borrowed against it, and what our tax returns looked like. In short, it wasn't really loaning us money based on our business plan, or the value and potential of our company. It wanted to know what collateral we could offer, and they made its decision based on that. We knew there had to be a better way, but we weren't sure what it was.

When startups approach venture capitalists for funding, they create a roadshow presentation, designed to communicate why their company is a good investment. The presentation typically includes an introduction of the management team, the vision for the company, the business plan, P&L statements and projections for the future with evidence to support them. After receiving some expert coaching from a colleague, we decided to create a mini-roadshow presentation for our local mid-market banks.

Our coach explained that we had been dealing with the lowest level bank representatives who were only capable of evaluating our assets as potential collateral for a loan. He shared that there was a next level of banker who would be able to look at our backgrounds and experience, our business plan, and our P&L statements, and see that we were creditworthy based on the growth and profitability of One Horn and the soundness of our plan. These bankers would be able to authorize much larger lines of credit at more favorable rates.

We began our presentation with our personal backgrounds, including our education and time in corporate America, and our business pivots up to that point. We were able to demonstrate that the primary reason we needed business credit was to cover the gap between when we received payment from a shipper, and when our truckers needed to be paid.

This gap grew significantly as we shifted to the freight agent model, and as our business volume increased. Rather than borrowing to buy land or equipment, we were borrowing solely to support revenue-generating activities. Our agents—most of whom have books of business worth a million dollars or more—

had to be confident we could handle a delayed payment without paying the truckers late.

Our business model showed the bank that if they extended us more credit, we could float many more loads, which would enable us to attract and keep the best agents. This empowered the agents to grow their businesses, which enabled us to grow One Horn. The higher-tier bank representatives understood this, and offered us credit based on this information, rather than on the value of our personal assets.

These bankers also understood that our business model made the typical requirement of a "cleanup period"—one month during the year when the bank expected us to have our balance completely paid off—didn't make sense for One Horn. When Cheryl explained that in order to comply with the cleanup period requirement, we would have to virtually halt our business growth, the representative removed the requirement. Having access to this level of banker made all the difference in the world.

The first time we did our mini-roadshow, we got one offer for three times the size of our existing credit line. The second time we did it—a few years later after a great deal of growth—we got three competitive offers. This led, somewhat ironically, to the angry banker hanging up on Cheryl.

Our access to good credit has enabled us to serve our agents at a much higher level. Some brokerages offer varying lines of credit to their agents' shippers, depending on how they perceive the agents' shippers' creditworthiness. But we have decided to make credit a yes or no question. If we choose to do business with an agent, we want that person's business to grow, so we offer no limit on the loads we will float. This policy enabled us to add one of our top performing agents, who, as we mentioned, left a brokerage because it would not provide him with sufficient credit to ship for a Fortune 500 company.

We are deeply grateful to have access to credit that is guaranteed by our business, and only indirectly by us personally. People have pointed out to us that we could now theoretically borrow a lot of money and take a chance with it. But this kind of risky and ill-advised behavior has never appealed to us. It's just not in our nature. Perhaps this is because we do not view the credit as "ours" as much as we view it as One Horn's. We own One Horn, but we are also its stewards, charged with steering it in the right direction and serving our agents and their customers in the best way possible.

CHAPTER 17

....

HAVE SCANNER, WILL TRAVEL

As we've already mentioned, *The Four-Hour Workweek* by Tim Ferriss inspired both Louis and me to make some adjustments to One Horn. One of Ferriss's themes is the idea that instead of running ourselves ragged for decades and then retiring, we should take "mini-retirements" throughout our lives, while we are still young enough to enjoy them. He also asserts that not only is travel pleasant, but it also refreshes the soul and boosts creativity.

Family travel was one of the main reasons we decided to become entrepreneurs, so these concepts really resonated with us. We wanted to have the freedom to see the world with our young children, as well as with each other. Of course, we still work on One Horn more than four hours a week. But by taking cues from Ferriss's book, we have greatly reduced the burden of running our company, which has enabled us to travel at least eight weeks out of the year. As Louis likes to say, we read *The Four-Hour Workweek* like a cookbook, choosing the recipes that appealed to us the most.

Ferriss's model doesn't work for everyone. Obviously, the owners of restaurants, retail stores, and doctors' offices can only work four hours a week if they are profitable enough to pay someone else to work for them. But cell phones and the internet have made all of us far more mobile than we used to be, and we can all take steps to take advantage of that flexibility.

Make Your Business Mobile

When a friend of mine who is a financial advisor took her

kids to the beach for a month, I was astounded. How was she able to run her business from North Carolina for four full weeks? She was one of the first people I knew who had successfully applied one of Ferriss's key recommendations, which is to make your business mobile.

So Louis and I decided to go away for two weeks and see how it went. We packed our Nissan Cube with a personal computer, scanner, and all the other One Horn essentials, and headed out for fourteen days of fun in the sun. We were quite the spectacle, unpacking an entire office from our car and lugging it up to our fourth-floor walkup apartment!

To prepare to take your business on the road for a week, start with what you would do to get away for a day. (And if you can't get away from your business for a day, you have a serious problem!) Steps like forwarding phone calls and getting emails on your phone or laptop are pretty straightforward. The other factors keeping you dependent on your physical location can include mailing supplies, office equipment, and physical inventory if applicable.

After you've made these basic arrangements, ask yourself these questions:

Which tasks can be done ahead of time or postponed until we get back?

Sales, marketing, and other tasks that are important but not extremely time sensitive, can easily be put off for a week. These are aspects of your business that shouldn't be neglected for long, but they can certainly be set aside temporarily. Luckily for me, this was more my territory than Louis's.

Of course, you don't really want to go away for a week and come back to two weeks' worth of work, which would negate a lot of the benefit of your time away. To avoid this, look for tasks that can be completed ahead of time. For example, I was able to preload my blogs before we left, and publish them with a click of a button whenever I wanted. Whenever possible, also try to automate, delegate, or do tasks remotely so you won't have to deal with them when you get back.

Which essential tasks can be done remotely?

In our case, billing was essential. For a while, we had an employee who could handle invoicing in Louis's absence. But we could also do it remotely with our scanner and personal computer. Unfortunately, the first time we tried this, it still took Louis many hours to get it done. Nevertheless, this ended up being a useful exercise, because it showed us clearly how we could make the process more efficient.

The first time we were away, we were able to preprint most of our checks and mail them from North Carolina. This worked fine, except for the last minute quick pay checks we offered carriers, 5 percent for a three-day turnaround, which still took a fair amount of time. But then we engaged the company in Connecticut to handle check printing, so it didn't matter where we were. Needless to say, Louis has had a much better time on vacation since then!

Moving Stratebo into the Cloud was also essential for making One Horn mobile. Even when you're working from a laptop, if the host server is located at your physical office, you risk disruption if the power goes out or something else happens back home. Ultimately, taking steps that enable you and your employees to work remotely can only help your business become more flexible and scalable.

Which essential tasks can be delegated to someone else?

Some tasks must be done at your physical location but can be temporarily delegated to someone else. The first time we got away, we had a friend pick up our mail for us, and deposit the checks that arrived. Depending on your business, you might be able to delegate extra responsibility to your employees, or even hire temporary workers, or a virtual assistant to take over certain basic tasks. Delegating also forces you to ensure your systems are clear and efficient. When you have to explain your processes to someone else who isn't used to the way you do things, you may uncover some steps that could be simplified or streamlined.

Once you have figured out how to go away for a week, it's just a few more steps to be able to go away for a month. Louis and I have been able to get away to resorts while our kids were at camp, while just checking our email once or twice a day. Our goals is always to enjoy new location without having too much work pile up while we are gone.

Making your business mobile is not a one-time event, but a gradual process. You'll remember from Chapter 4, "From Surviving to Thriving," that Louis has a special headset that fits inside his ski helmet so he can take customer calls when necessary. Before he developed this solution, he actually used to ski with a laptop in his backpack, and later with a tablet. Each time you go away, you'll learn more about how to make your business processes more efficient and mobile.

Living the Life You Want Now

As we've already mentioned, a huge motivation for buying One Horn in the first place was the ability to live the life we wanted to live now, instead of after we retired. Of course this means different things to different people. We love to ski; spending the day in fresh air, getting exercise and talking to our kids on the chairlift is just about the best thing ever for us. But others might enjoy hiking, sailing, golf, or other enriching recreational activities.

People in more traditional employment situations also find rest and refreshment in their vacations. But as entrepreneurs, we have traded off some of our income security and predictability for more control over our schedules. Yet some entrepreneurs are just as chained to their businesses as they would be in a traditional job. What is the point of having control of our schedules if we are not filling them with activities we enjoy?

Not long ago, Louis was out playing golf with some friends. During the eighteen holes, he took three short phone calls to resolve some issues that happened to come up while he was out. His friends initially felt bad for him, because they assumed he couldn't get away from his work even for a day. But after chatting about it, they realized that Louis wasn't taking the day off the way they were; he was just having another typical "day at the office," which happened to be out on the golf course.

Louis's friends were working at a breakneck pace week after week, and this golf outing was a welcome rest where they turned off their phones and put their jobs completely out of their minds. But Louis had the freedom to work at a more leisurely pace whenever he wanted to. It wasn't that he never spent intense time coding, just as I would sometimes spend very focused times developing marketing plans or communications; but the pace and intensity are almost always our choice.

It's worth mentioning that we never could have worked from the beach the first year or two we were in business. Besides the fact that we were an asset-based company and dependent on our physical location, we were also just learning the ropes. Only when we had paid our dues and learned our industry well were we able to automate enough so that we could relax whenever we wished.

Malcolm Gladwelll's famous 10,000-hour rule, detailed in his 2008 book *Outliers,* reminds us that even the most talented people have to invest a great deal of hard work before they master their craft. After thousands of hours of running One Horn, we know our industry, our customers, and our bank account balances inside and out. And that has enabled us to live the life we've always wanted.

CHAPTER 18

·····················

PRIORITIZE, ORGANIZE, BUNDLE BEST PRACTICES

Recruiting

Operations

Accounting

Many small businesses get more and more disorganized as they grow. When you don't have a fulltime staff devoted to filing and other administrative duties, it's very easy for the papers and the electronic clutter to pile up. Before long, this can make for a stressful and chaotic environment where important tasks are falling through the cracks.

Just like strategic planning, organization is something that you must make time for in the short term so that you can benefit from it in the long term. If you don't, chronic disorganization may cost you several hours a day looking for things you have misplaced, or attacking tasks in a haphazard manner. There are many different methods of organization that work well. The most important thing is to choose a method that you are comfortable with.

The method that worked for me is outlined in David Allen's book *Getting Things Done: The Art of Stress-Free Productivity*. As the title suggests, Allen's approach puts stress reduction in the forefront of organizational strategy. This was perfect for Cheryl and for me, since both of us make better decisions and enjoy life more when we are less stressed out.

Sorting and Prioritizing

When you work at a traditional job, it may be possible to write a single to-do list for the day, depending on how narrow your duties are. But when you are an entrepreneur, you wear a dozen different hats in the course of a week. Cheryl and I were the accountants, IT support, sales representatives, collections agents, and marketing directors for One Horn, all rolled into one (or two, really). Writing out one to-do list made it difficult to determine which task deserved our attention at any given moment.

Sorting the items on your to-do list by category—which for me might involve categories like accounting, coding, outside projects, and so on—can help you begin to prioritize and attack your list systematically. Start by labeling each task or document and filing it, either in a physical folder, or in a file folder on your computer, tablet, or phone. Then move on to the next item.

Once your categories are set, you need to prioritize. Most of us understand the concept of prioritizing. Stephen Covey's four quadrants work as well any method to categorize tasks. They are:

	Urgent	Not Urgent
Important	1 (emergencies)	2 (marketing/ strategizing)
Not Important	3 (interruptions)	4 (trivial and wasteful activities)

The trick to prioritizing is to examine the tasks you typically encounter in a given day or week, and decide ahead of time which category they fall into.

Generally speaking, each communication you receive— whether by phone, email, or any other method—represents an open task. While there are plenty of programs and applications that sort your emails into different folders, you must decide which senders fall into which of those four quadrants, and tell the program what to do.

Cheryl and I decided to categorize our customers by A, B, and C priority. This was nothing personal, but simply related to how important their business was to ours. A problem involving an "A" customer was important and urgent; we would drop everything and deal with it right away. A problem from a "B" customer would be dealt with before the end of the day, and a problem from a "C" customer before the end of the week or so. We had our software sort the emails accordingly, and we check the "A" priority folder multiple times a day, the "B" folder two or three times a day, and the "C" folder once a day.

Important and urgent tasks for One Horn also included recruiting. When our kids were in elementary school, they participated in Read Across America Day (also Dr. Seuss's birthday). On that date, they followed an acronym, DEAR, which stood for: "Drop Everything and Read." Cheryl and I developed a similar saying: "Drop Everything and Recruit." While there might not have been a fixed deadline by which we needed to persuade another agent to come work for us, it was absolutely central to revenue generation and growth. In practical terms, this meant we responded very quickly to candidates who expressed interest in our brokerage, which made us more competitive in the recruiting process.

Many entrepreneurs also find it useful to analyze their day and identify what they actually do with all the hours. When Cheryl and I did this, we actually wrote down everything we did all day in fifteen-minute increments for two weeks. Besides minimizing and eliminating distractions, this exercise helped us identify what took up the most time. Then we were able to attack the most time-consuming or inefficient tasks first.

Sometimes you will also uncover a flaw in your processes or systems that generates emergencies on a regular basis. For example, if there is a problem in our software coding that generates an error every fifteen loads, we will find ourselves forced to fix the problem manually each time it comes up. But if we take the time to fix the original error, we are saving time down the road. If something is constantly demanding your immediate attention, ask yourself what you can do about it. As a business leader, fighting fires should not be one of your primary activities.

After reading *Procrastinate on Purpose* by Rory Vaden, Cheryl and I added another dimension to the way we prioritize: significance. How much does a particular task matter, and how long will it matter into the future? Some things we do today may not seem urgent, but they can greatly increase our efficiency in the future, which means they are well worth tackling sooner than later. Significant tasks could include teaching and training employees, or in our case, investing time into automation.

Priorities aren't static. Just as your family's needs change over time, depending on the age of your children and other unpredictable factors, so the needs of your business will change with the development of your systems and shifts in the market. We like to keep weekly tabs on how our agents and customers are doing, ensuring that we are offering help and praise where appropriate. We also host an annual agent retreat where we gather for in-person meetings, dinners, and socializing. This helps us keep a finger on the pulse of our business and identify where we may need to adjust our priorities.

Managing Energy

As we've said, even though we run a largely automated company that allows us to travel eight weeks a year and ski to our hearts' content, there are still things that neither of us like to do. I like to bundle all of these tasks together for what I call Crap Day Friday, when I knock them all out at once. Cheryl prefers to take care of hers on Thursday afternoons after lunch. Some people might like to do theirs on Monday morning and get them out of the way.

Undesirable tasks may be mindless and annoying, or they can really drain your energy. Sometimes it may make sense to hire someone to do them, as we covered in Chapter 11, "Outsourcing." (We still opt to do some of these tasks ourselves, because they really take very little time.) You may want to reward yourself with a treat—an energizing snack, a short walk, a quick chat with a friend—to help keep yourself motivated to complete them.

Cheryl has found it particularly helpful to assess and manage her energy level throughout the day. She has found, like many of us, that she has the most mental energy in the morning, so she reserves that time for the tasks demanding the most concentration. Back when she had to do sales for One Horn, she would block off 10:00 AM to noon for cold calling.

This was not her favorite job, so it was also helpful to get it out of the way early.

We have both learned that the amount of time it takes to focus on a task after an interruption makes blocking off ninety uninterrupted minutes to work on something a much more efficient use of our time. Some might ask why they should not reserve six to ten hours of interrupted time? But this does not actually work for most people. Warren Rustand, a speaker at an EO event, once compared pacing yourself in your work to the way athletes participate in interval training, alternating periods of exertion with short breaks for rest and recovery. Cheryl often will work for ninety minutes, and then rise to make a cup of tea or put in a load of laundry.

The need for periodic recovery and refreshment also illustrates why it is often better to break down large projects—like getting organized—into smaller, more manageable pieces. If a project drags on for months, it can seem interminable. Yet smaller projects that actually get finished provide a sense of satisfaction, as well as a burst of energy and confidence that you can reinvest into the next task.

In their October 2007 article in *Harvard Business Review,* "Manage Your Energy, Not Your Time," authors Tony Schwartz and Catherine McCarthy explained, "The core problem with working longer hours is that time is a finite resource. Energy is a different story. Defined in physics as the capacity to work, energy comes from four main wellsprings in human beings: the body, emotions, mind, and spirit. In each, energy can be systematically expanded and regularly renewed by establishing specific rituals—behaviors that are intentionally practiced and precisely scheduled, with the goal of making them unconscious and automatic as quickly as possible."

All of us have days when we struggle to get going, or when nothing seems to be going well. We have a friend who advises that on days like that, you should try to stop struggling and do one useful thing. It could be sending an email, paying a bill, making a phone call, or even emptying the dishwasher. The satisfaction from getting one useful task out of the way is often enough to get you back on track.

It's also important to remember that while the interval training and energy management approaches will typically yield healthy productivity, there are some tasks that are so cognitively demanding that they require larger blocks of uninterrupted time. In his book *Deep Work*, Cal Newport makes the case for cultivating the ability to concentrate intensely for longer periods of time. This has been vital to me in my coding work and has benefited Cheryl tremendously as she studied for her business coaching certification. Ultimately, the capacity for such extended focus can benefit almost anyone in any profession.

Again, your particular method of organization for your time, documents, and tasks doesn't really matter. You just need to pick a method that works for you. If you haven't gotten started yet, take a weekend to read a book or two on organization, and then get going. Work at it deliberately and consistently. Each time you make progress, your success will increase your confidence that you can tackle the next problem.

PART THREE
LIFE LESSONS

CHAPTER 19

WOMAN IN A MAN'S INDUSTRY

As a little girl, my family and I were the first African Americans to purchase a home in our neighborhood. It was such an unusual occurrence that our new neighbors sent their children over to check us out. Those were very different times, and my parents—who were both educated professionals—still had many career paths closed to them because of their race.

Yet despite the obstacles my parents faced, they raised me to believe that every generation would make progress over the previous generation. They both had master's degrees from top universities, and taught me that with the strong foundation of a good education, I could do anything I wanted with my life. My parents' love for and faith in me gave me a strong sense of self-confidence. It simply never occurred to me that I couldn't do anything I wanted in business or life.

Going to school, I knew I would have to work extremely hard to prove myself to my teachers and classmates. I ended up becoming the valedictorian of my high school graduating class, and going on to success in Ivy League undergraduate and graduate schools. Learning to rise to the challenges before me, instead of complaining about the unfairness of life, prepared me well to be a woman in trucking and transportation, which is a male-dominated industry. Rather than feel intimidated or overwhelmed, I have always kept in mind that nearly every industry was once completely dominated by men. Women have successfully come into their own in medicine, law, and countless other fields. So why not trucking?

Leveraging Your Strengths

My experience in male dominated industries isn't limited to trucking. As a nineteen-year-old college student, I had an internship on the trading floor of a major investment banking firm that was probably over 80 percent men. I quickly got used to being one of just a few women around.

After completing my undergraduate degree at Cornell, I went into investment banking full time. (Although I didn't experience much overt discrimination, I did notice that men seemed to get promoted much faster.) And after my time in marketing, which had more women in the field (although mostly men at the top), Louis and I bought One Horn.

All these experiences taught me that being a woman in a man's industry can be a distinct advantage if you learn to leverage your strengths. For example, you are automatically more memorable in a networking situation if the room is full of men. As long as you are confident, take initiative, and carry yourself like you belong there, you will typically be very well received. You may even find that many men prefer to talk to a woman if they've just spent the last hour talking to other guys.

Women have plenty of natural strengths that we can leverage in a business environment. Many of the women I have known in my career had strong interpersonal skills and tended to be better listeners and more organized than our male counterparts. In trucking and transportation, for example, female agents I've observed often were able to listen to a frustrated trucker and talk him through unexpected challenges very effectively.

Most women are great at building strong relationships. This helps us figure out what clients actually need and deliver on what we promise. It also helps us smooth over situations where a little empathy and compassion can go a long way. These are valuable skills in a multitude of industries and fields.

Although we may bring a different set of leadership strengths to the table, we still have to demonstrate that we know as much or more than our male counterparts in order to get the same opportunities. Complaining about this reality gets us absolutely nowhere. Once we accept it and choose to excel with style and grace, we will make much more progress toward our goals.

Think Like a Man?

Over the years, many have asserted that women need to act like men in order to compete with them professionally. We have been encouraged to dress in power suits, be aggressive, and suppress any overtly feminine qualities. Eighties fashion trends, such as shoulder pads and ties for women's business suits exemplified these ideas.

While I disagree that women need to become masculine in order to succeed in business (or in any profession), I do think there are a few areas where we can take cues from our male friends, colleagues and family members. First of all, during my days in corporate America I noticed that many of the men with whom I worked really excelled in self-promotion, whereas I encountered fewer women with that particular skill. For example, if there is a position open at a company with five qualifications listed in the job description, most women—in my experience—will not apply unless they possess all five qualifications. Many men, on the other hand, will apply even if they only possess two. In these situations, I typically advise women to think like a man and go for it. You'll never know unless you try!

Some women also struggle to assert themselves, particularly in situations involving conflict. Due to biased social norms, women tend to be perceived more negatively in conflict than men are. My advice to women in these situations is to be honest and direct, while never getting visibly upset. Develop a thick skin, and do whatever you have to do to appear calm and in complete control of your emotions. (Vent about it to a friend later if you must!) You simply will not be taken seriously at work if you are unable to maintain a professional demeanor regardless of the situation.

Even though I always tried to keep my emotions in check, there were times while I was in corporate America that I allowed my overall displeasure with my situation to show through. One of my former bosses pulled me aside and advised me that "perception is reality." He meant that the way people in power perceived me was their reality. Even if I was doing a great job, my supervisors' ability to perceive my underlying discontentment would negatively affect their opinion of me and my work.

Lastly, women need to be ready and eager to participate in traditionally male activities. These could include golf (yes, I'm still taking lessons!), watching sports, or just getting a drink after work on Fridays. Professionals often do important relationship building outside of work, and women miss out when we don't participate.

During my investment banking days, I always made it a point to hang out with my coworkers after work on Fridays. Sure, I was the only woman (and I was quite a bit younger than everyone else), but I just didn't let it bother me. Not only were my coworkers protective of me—like good older brothers— but they also taught me a lot during those times. When they realized how curious and eager I was to learn, they even let me start day trading a little. I know if I hadn't been willing to bond with them this way, I would have missed out on a lot.

Paying it Forward

There was a time when there were so few professional opportunities open to women that they often felt they could not afford to display any interest in family or other traditionally feminine pursuits, nor offer any career help to other women. While a few people may still possess this toxic mindset, most of us have thankfully concluded that there are now more than enough opportunities for everyone to excel.

For this reason, I have always taken pleasure in mentoring younger women in business, whether it's my own daughter, the daughters of friends, or women I encounter in my professional life. I also accept public speaking opportunities when I can, so I am able share my experiences and ideas in the hope that they will help others. I have benefited from so many wonderful female and male speakers, writers, and thinkers, that I want to help as many as I can.

As of this writing, I have spoken at places like Columbia Business School, Rutgers Business School, Montclair University,

The Association for Corporate Growth, and at the New Jersey Association of Women Business Owners, to name a few. I cover a variety of topics, including entrepreneurship and women in business. For women starting their own businesses, my best advice is to develop a strong plan, write down specific measurable goals, as well as consult people in their industry who have successfully been down the path.

I counsel women on the corporate track to develop a clear vision for where they want their careers to take them. This helps them evaluate each new opportunity to determine if it will help them make progress toward their goals. Otherwise, it is easy to make certain decisions—because of salary or position, for example—that may actually pull them away from what they ultimately want to achieve.

In addition, I urge all women not to be afraid to adjust their visions and goals if their priorities change, as mine did. I have no doubt I could have achieved my original goal of rising very high in a very large company, but just because you are capable of doing something doesn't mean you have to do it. You can always reinvent yourself or your career if you're not content with who you are and what you're doing. I've personally made at least three major career changes, moving from finance to marketing to entrepreneurship to business coaching.

I am extremely grateful to have both a great family and a great business. I am also glad that our culture has progressed to the point where I (and all the young women coming up in the professional world) don't have to pretend that we only care about our careers in order to be successful. I believe that any woman can succeed at anything she puts her mind to as long as she is strong, determined, capable, and willing to learn.

CHAPTER 20

IT'S TRUCKING, NOT OUR CALLING

IT'S TRUCKING, NOT OUR CALLING

When I was growing up, I don't remember hearing any advice about finding my calling. Consequently, I never worried about figuring out that one thing I could do better than anyone else, or discovering something I was so passionate about that it didn't feel like work. My parents grew up in a time when they were thankful to be able to obtain professional jobs. Their goals were the same as almost all of humanity's have been from time immemorial: to provide for their family as well as they possibly could.

But we live in an era of unprecedented prosperity—at least in many parts of the world—and so now we want to do more than just provide our families with food, shelter and clothing. We want to find meaning and purpose in our work. We want to discover more about ourselves in what we do. These are wonderful goals, but they can be taken too far. Just as you do not want to sacrifice your personal life for a career, it's probably not a good idea to sacrifice your family's material security in pursuit of your "calling" if you can't make a living doing it.

Both Louis and I originally pursued professions based primarily on what we thought we were good at, and would enable us to earn enough money to support ourselves as independent adults, and later would provide comfort and security for our eventual family. But as you know by now, we both became quickly disillusioned with the sacrifices those professions were requiring of us. We did not become entrepreneurs because we thought trucking was our calling. We became entrepreneurs to be able to have the freedom to both provide for our family and have control over our schedules.

Many people look for their calling by examining the activities where they experience what is often called peak performance or "flow." Like a basketball player "in the zone,"—a mental state where the basket looks larger and the game appears to be taking place in slow motion—it feels amazing to crank out ten thousand words on your laptop in a single sitting, electrify a crowd with a speech, or create a work of art that moves and inspires the masses. It's easy to see why people want their vocations to give them this kind of sensation every day.

Yet many people who experience this kind of exhilarating feeling are unable to monetize the activity that brings it, especially early in their careers. For every financially successful musician, there are thousands of others struggling to make ends meet, or simply performing as a hobby. Some people choose to struggle financially their entire lives, because it is very important to them to make a living in a particular way. We chose to focus on the life we wanted, and make our work considerations, whether exhilarating or not, supportive of that. This didn't mean we were closed to the idea of pursuing a calling; it simply wasn't our top priority.

We are not particularly passionate about the operational side of transportation, but that doesn't mean we do not enjoy many aspects of owning and running One Horn. We do. I love interacting with our great team of freight agents, writing blogs, recruiting, marketing our business, and coming up with new strategies. Louis deeply enjoys coding, business process reengineering, and problem solving. These are activities we would enjoy if we did them for any company, but the fact that we have created such a warm, supportive environment for ourselves and our associates is definitely an added bonus.

But as we've mentioned, there were also things that needed to be done—particularly during the early years of the business—that neither of us liked much. I did not care for sales or collections, and Louis didn't particularly enjoy dispatching, but we did these activities until we found a way not to have to do them anymore. If we had given up on One Horn because of these temporarily annoying tasks, we would have missed out on the benefits we have now. (We also would have gone bankrupt!)

So although we don't look at running One Horn as our calling, we used it as an opportunity to move closer and closer to our dream jobs. As we gradually automated the parts of the business we don't enjoy, we found our days filled with more of the things we do enjoy. But ultimately, we prioritized the dream life over the dream job.

For almost all of us, work will occupy more of our time than anything else, so we definitely don't want to spend our lives doing something we really don't like. But there is more to life than work. Rather than simply listing the qualities of your dream job (or your dream duties in your business), why not also list the qualities of your dream life?

Louis and I both did this, and fortunately for us, our lists were very similar. As you know by now, family travel has always been very important to both of us, with skiing at the top of the list. We also enjoy hiking and golf, and attending cultural events. I have always wanted to make time for things like yoga and meditation.

While we've never needed to drive luxury cars that turn heads or wear clothes from the runways of Paris and Milan, we have always wanted enough time to exercise daily and to enjoy high quality, delicious food and wine on a regular basis. And as you know both Louis and I wanted to spend regular quality time together as a couple, with our kids and with our good friends. Running One Horn enabled us to do almost all these things, while spending most of our work time doing things we enjoy.

But the truly amazing part is that running One Horn also opened the door for both of us to discover and pursue our true callings. Louis has always found programming extremely gratifying, and launching Stratebo as a Software as a Service (SaaS) has enabled him to monetize that passion. Running One Horn enabled me to build up what Cal Newport calls in his book *So Good They Can't Ignore You*—"career capital," an area of proficiency that is highly valuable to others. I became an expert in growth and strategy, which poised me perfectly to become a certified business coach, my true passion. This is something I never could have done right out of business school, because I simply didn't have the experience or credibility. So while we focused on building our dream lives, we were extremely fortunate to end up in our dream jobs as well.

CHAPTER 21

....

ALL IN THE FAMILY

ALL IN THE FAMILY

Afew years ago, Cheryl and I attended a presentation given by a local firm on the challenges of running a family business. Up until that point, we had assumed that One Horn was a family business, because Cheryl and I are family, and it's our business. But listening to this presentation changed our perspective on that forever.

The firm in question was run by a married couple who also employed their adult children. The wife shared briefly about one of their typical conflicts: a debate over how large a bonus they could give to one of their sons, so he could take his family to Disney World. Cheryl and I listened to this story and stared at each other in disbelief.

We realized in that moment that One Horn was not a family business in the way that this company was. Although we owned One Horn and had employed our children and even Cheryl's mother at various times, we never would have made a salary or a bonus decision based on their personal needs or desires. Furthermore, we had no succession plan to hand the business over to our children once they reached a certain age. We expect them to make their own way in the world, just as we did. But certainly as parents, we are doing all we can to ensure they have the tools and resources they need to chart their own paths.

This is a very important distinction, because some children who grow up in a family business feel pressure to follow in their parents' footsteps. (I should add here that Alexander and Genevieve have never expressed any interest in taking over

One Horn!) Other children may plan their careers around the assumption that they will inherit or take over the reins of the business at a certain point in the future. We have known some parents who make this commitment to a child only to realize that they weren't quite ready to stop working when the time came. Still other parents make the commitment and then discover that their children are not well-suited to run the business without their oversight.

None of this is to say that a plan of succession with one or more children taking over a business might not be the right decision for some families. When the children share both their parents' aptitude for running the business, and also share their interest and desire to do so, a plan of succession may make the most sense. But that is not what we chose. One Horn is what we refer to as a "closely held" company, not a family business in the most traditional sense.

Entrepreneurship and Parenting

"What are we supposed to do now?"

Like many new parents, this was the question Cheryl and I asked each other when we brought our first child Alexander home from the hospital. We learned on the job, as everyone does, but we missed our children terribly during those early years when we were not home very much. One Horn enabled us to have more hours with our children, which gave us more time not only to enjoy them, but also to teach them what we wanted them to know.

There are some notable similarities in the way we approach

running our business and raising our kids. Just as we wanted to create an efficient business that could run without excessive input from us, we wanted to raise responsible and self-reliant children. Although we did teach them to do certain tasks for the business, our main goal was to teach them skills for life. This included everything from doing their own laundry and emptying the dishwasher without being told, to setting goals for themselves and making a plan to achieve them.

Working from home also enabled us to share life and business lessons with our kids as we went about our day. They definitely learned a lot about concepts like revenue, expenses, and profit at an early age. In addition to seeing the perks of working for ourselves, they had a front row seat for the challenges. We were very honest with them about both our successes and our failures, which enabled them to see firsthand how we overcame obstacles.

We also involve both Alexander and Genevieve in the creative process by sharing our new ideas and updating them on how things are going. While the details of each little experiment we try might not be directly applicable to their future careers, they have learned a great deal about how to tackle and solve problems effectively. Perhaps most importantly, they have watched us weather the ups and downs with a good attitude.

Many of our adulthood habits are formed by watching our parents. Our kids know how to cut back on spending when money is tight, and to spend responsibly even when times are good, because they have seen us do these things. They are both careful about saving money and never demand or request frivolous purchases from us. Naturally, there are some skills that are a work in progress. Unsurprisingly, not every chore is completed perfectly every time. But overall, we feel they are well on their way to becoming responsible and self-reliant adults.

Dealing with Challenges

Although working from home benefited our family tremendously, we still had to balance work and parenting responsibilities. There were certainly occasions when the children interrupted Cheryl and me while we were working, but these were much rarer than you might think. For the most part the kids understood that work was important and were careful to ask if it was a good time before they came into either of our offices. They also understood that I, in particular, needed quiet in order to code, and they were almost always very considerate of this.

The biggest challenge with noise or distractions typically came when they had friends over. However, for the most part, they were able to get their friends to keep quiet near our offices. I cannot recall a single time when I had a problematic level of noise on my end of a phone conversation as a result of the children. Our success in these areas came mostly from the normal boundary setting that all parents must do with their children. Children will typically rise to their parents' expectations, as long as parents consistently enforce the rules.

Every choice in life involves tradeoffs, and owning your own business is no exception. Just as Alexander and Genevieve have a great deal of insight into the ups and downs of working for yourself, they do not have as much firsthand understanding of the benefits and restrictions associated with being in the traditional workforce. However, these are things they can learn on their own as they launch their own careers. Whatever path they choose in the end, we are confident they will find success.

CHAPTER 22

· · · · · · · · · · · · · · · · · ·

MARRIED COUPLE WORKING TOGETHER

MARRIED COUPLE WORKING TOGETHER

As you know by now, Louis and I love to give back to other entrepreneurs through speaking, writing and mentoring. Not surprisingly, the most common questions we receive relate to how we grew our business tenfold in the midst of a historic recession. But a close second would be the question of how we manage to run a business together as a married couple without driving each other crazy!

As we've already covered, we were extremely fortunate to enter our marriage with very similar values, particularly regarding money and spending. This has been incredibly helpful in minimizing conflict and enabling us to make decisions together. But working together has also taught us a lot about ourselves, our marriage and our family as a whole.

Are You Sure You Want to Work with Your Wife?

When Louis and I decided to buy One Horn, Louis was shocked at how many people expressed concern over the idea that he would be working with me full time. It simply never occurred to either of us that this would be an issue. Yet many of our married friends assured us that they could never work together all day without it negatively affecting their relationship.

Marriages are as varied as individuals. Some people marry right out of school and do a lot of their growing up as a couple. Others establish their careers first, and may develop very different preferences before they settle down and build a life together. Some, like Louis and me, want to spend as much time together as possible, while others find that "absence makes the heart grow fonder."

While marriages work in all sorts of ways, some basic factors are necessary for any successful working relationship. Open, honest, respectful communication has been absolutely essential to our ability to work well together. In addition to daily conversations about our most pressing decisions, our hot tub strategy sessions are regular opportunities to communicate about longer-term goals and ideas. These discussions ensure that we are on the same page.

Great communication builds relationships that are strong enough to weather conflict. Although we don't disagree often, we naturally have our fair share of difficult days. We always try our best to be sensitive to one another and offer encouragement when needed. We also work hard not to take out our frustrations on each other.

A degree of awareness and acceptance of your own strengths and weaknesses—as well as those of your spouse—also goes a long way. We have long known that Louis is an introvert and I am an extrovert, so he is very content being alone, while I derive energy from being with others. This knowledge helps us each understand why the other may respond to various situations differently. Louis has often shielded me from some of the smaller issues with customers or vendors, because he knows they will upset me more than they will bother him. Likewise, I know that some marketing and sales situations make Louis uncomfortable, so I take the lead on those.

Naturally we celebrate each other's successes, just as we would if we both worked in traditional environments. I may not understand all the ins and outs of coding, but I am always excited when Louis solves a problem. In the same way, Louis may be unsure of all the subtleties involved in a marketing campaign, but he is always thrilled when my strategies are successful.

When things don't go the way we'd hoped, we naturally feel disappointed. But we work hard not to allow disappointment to degenerate into blame. Instead, we try to accept what has happened and focus on the solutions and adjustments that make sense.

In his book *The Four Agreements: A Practical Guide to Personal Freedom*, Don Miguel Ruiz urges his readers not to make assumptions in their relationships. Many conflicts are simply the result of misunderstandings. On the rare occasions Louis and I do disagree, we have found that asking one another for clarification often resolves the issue. We also tend to defer to one another if one of us feels strongly about something, and we are very fortunate that we almost never feel strongly in opposite directions.

Overall, we try to treat each other with the same respect we would in a professional environment, even if we don't use the same level of formality. We have faced all sorts of challenges, just as we did when we both worked in corporate America. But ultimately, our respect for one another's time, needs, and preferences has enabled us to work together productively, while strengthening our personal relationship.

Strategies for Success

In addition to caring for our marriage, we also took several practical steps to set up our working relationship for success. First, our decision to have completely separate work spaces. This decision was really driven by our mutual need to be productive, rather than by a concern that we would get on each other's nerves. We love to chat, and we both recognized that we would probably not get too much done if we shared an office.

While Louis was doing dispatching, he had to be on the phone for much of the day, which would have made it very difficult for me to get much work done. Likewise, he would have had trouble coding while I was cold calling or listening to music while I worked. Louis also prefers a minimalistic workspace, while my walls are filled with our daughter Genevieve's art and other things that inspire me.

Second, we have always tried to divide the tasks neither of us like, such as finance, and billing, as evenly as possible between us. When we are working on something together—a sales presentation for example—we take the time to clarify who will take the lead on which parts. Rather than one of us typing and the other one looking over his or her shoulder, we have found it much more effective to divide the tasks and send our work to each other for feedback.

Third, as we mentioned in the previous section, we do our best to respect each other's time, work nstyles and needs. I am very careful not to interrupt Louis when he is engrossed in something, and he does the same for me. I am most comfortable being very prepared for a sales presentation, whereas Louis tends to get things done very close to the deadline. So when we take on a joint project, we are sure to agree on deadlines ahead of time, working with each other's preferences. When Louis consults me on a technical problem, he is careful to present the pros and cons of each option in a way I can relate to, and I do the same for him in my areas of responsibility. This enables us both to understand each other and offer sound feedback.

Finally, while we don't have fixed hours when we will or won't talk about work, we do have some basic guidelines that we follow. Louis is a morning person, but I am not. He respects that by not bringing any work-related items to me until I am seated at my desk in the morning. Sometimes we are both happy to discuss business issues even after dinner, but other times one or both of us are ready to think about other things and leave work for the next morning.

Once in a while, we will drive into the city during rush hour and see the lines of cars waiting to enter the parking garage of a large office building. That spectacle reminds us why we do what we do. Marriage and running a business both offer their fair share of challenges to even the most mature people. Living our lives with a sense of gratitude—recognizing how good we really do have it—helps us keep perspective during the inevitable frustrations that occasionally arise.

CHAPTER 23

· · · · · · · · · · · · · · · · · · ·

WE STILL AVOID BUSES

"**W**hat would happen to your business if you got hit by a bus?" This is the classic question that entrepreneurs are asked to determine whether or not they have successfully developed an exit strategy that enables the business to run in their absence. Often owners of small or even medium-sized businesses are so involved in day-to-day operations that if they were to be removed from the situation, things would come to a grinding halt. The most common way to change this is by growing the business to the point where you can afford to hire a general manager or a CEO.

Setting up your business so that it can operate without you makes sense for both succession planning and for freedom. Once the business doesn't need you to make it through the day, you can take extended vacations and work only when you want. You can even sell and retire without missing a beat. Furthermore, most of us have heard horror stories of business owners actually dying without an exit plan. In these cases, relatives are often forced to spend months toiling over the books to wind everything down. A proper succession plan would have enabled the heirs to sell the business right away and benefit from—rather than be burdened by—everything the owner built.

Succession Planning

Although Louis and I take the issue of succession planning seriously, we have chosen not to remove ourselves from the day-to-day operations at One Horn. We have remained very much in charge, and we have not employed anyone else, although we do retain vendors for specific tasks. So in some ways, we have chosen to avoid "the bus question," by doing our best to mitigate the vulnerabilities our business would be exposed to in the absence of either of us.

Our reasons for staying at the helm are very straightforward: the amount of work required to run One Horn simply doesn't justify a fulltime employee. Even if it did, we would have a hard time finding someone with the combination of skills necessary to do what we do, and keep up with our somewhat unpredictable schedule. But that doesn't mean we have rejected the wisdom of ensuring our company could run without us if the need arose.

From very early on, we took the time to write out all our daily, weekly, and monthly tasks and procedures. We did this in part to make our systems more efficient, and to look for ways to eliminate and automate various components. But we also ensured everything was documented properly so that I could take over Louis's duties, or he could take over mine, if it ever became necessary.

This kind of documentation often feels impossible to complete during the early years of running a business. Days are typically hectic and unpredictable, and owners feel stretched to the limit. But don't put it off too long. Start by thinking through all your daily activities, writing down everything you do and the best way to do it. Then set aside time to record all of your weekly and monthly tasks. This doesn't have to be done all at once; just work on it periodically until it is complete. Lastly, you'll eventually want to document how to close out the books at the end of the year.

If you choose to hire a general manager to take over your duties, all this documentation will ensure that such a person knows exactly what to do. If you don't—and the bus finally comes for you—everything is written out so that others can take over your tasks and your heirs won't have too much trouble sorting through your affairs. We have strived to take all these precautions while still remaining actively involved in running our business, because running it really isn't much of a burden.

Looking Ahead

As long as we are in charge, we want One Horn to grow. In his book, *The Curve Ahead: Discovering the Path to Unlimited Growth*, author Dave Power observes that many companies stop growing long before they have reached their potential. Leaders of successful companies, on the other hand, never stop searching for the next innovation. The key, Power explains, is to discover ways to build innovation into the day-to-day rhythm of how we run our businesses.

For us, continual innovation has taken two major forms: improving our software and adjusting our business model. Remaining at the helm of One Horn without any employees has helped us stay extremely flexible in both these areas. Lower expenses enable us pay off debt and build cash reserves, while the absence of employees helps us pivot relatively easily.

Another key for our continual innovation has been our dedication to reading and studying, as well as attending seminars and other entrepreneurial and business gatherings. As we've mentioned, we take these activities seriously, always asking what information and insight we can apply to our business. And, as you might imagine, joining the Gazelles Coaching Community has provided me with even more access to resources to help us innovate and grow. Devoting time to learning and personal enrichment also keeps our creative juices flowing, leading to new ideas of our own.

It would have been very easy for us to get comfortable once we had achieved the level of growth we were seeking. And that is what often happens with so many entrepreneurs who enjoy a measure of success. They begin planning the rest of their lives as if the profitable months they just experienced will extend indefinitely into the future.

The key lesson of all our pivots was not that we had arrived at the perfect formula for doing business forever. Each successful pivot just meant that we had found a formula that worked for our family under those particular market conditions. But those change, as do the needs of any family. So we have always tried to look toward the future, doing our best to evaluate what might come next and how to be ready for it.

When we first began One Horn, our children were four and seven years old. Like all young children, they needed extensive supervision and care. Investing in One Horn's systems and automation freed us up to do what we wanted to do for them as well as enjoy their company. As they grew, we also worked hard to teach them to be independent and self-sufficient. At the time of this writing, our son is in college and our daughter is a senior in high school who cooks dinner, cleans the kitchen, does her own laundry, and gets her schoolwork done without being told (almost). This has made us very proud and a tiny bit sad, since they no longer need us like they used to.

As our family needs have changed, so have our goals for running One Horn. We still run our company to serve our family—not the other way around—and our overall goal is still freedom. But now we can look forward to more vacation time and even more flexibility. We can choose to spend our time doing what we want to do, invest in our other businesses, and enjoy time with our kids when they choose to grace us with their presence!

Giving Back

As we've repeated throughout this book, we never would have gotten to where we are now without the encouragement and advice of so many wonderful friends and colleagues. In fact, Louis reflected recently how much less guidance he received when he was working in corporate America. Back then, he was managing a division of hundreds of employees and a budget of millions of dollars, but he would have undoubtedly accomplished so much more if he had had the support he has now.

We still meet regularly in our hot tub, thinking of new ways to keep One Horn growing and profitable, so our agents and our family can continue to thrive. In the meantime we're also developing our other "irons in the fire" with my coaching business and Louis's software company, mentioned in Chapter 8, "Diversifying the Family Interests." No venture is without its challenges and risks, but we feel extremely fortunate to have the work and home life that we do.

Every business owner will face challenges and obstacles to growth. It is so easy to lose perspective and become discouraged, especially when you are new to the game. Yet as you continue to grow and gain experience, you learn to focus and persevere. You will discover more about what freedom means to you, and how to secure it. With the right advisors, resources, and support, you will soon be comfortable, confident, and capable of reaching your goals, as well as secure in the business and the life you want.

BONUS CHAPTER

THE KIDS' PERSPECTIVE

THE KIDS' PERSPECTIVE

Throughout this book, you've read about how much we value family. Since you've heard from both of us quite a bit, we thought we'd give the last word to our kids themselves. After all, they were one of the most important motivating factors behind our decision to become entrepreneurs in the first place.

We had our good friend Carl Gould—whose voice you've heard if you've listened to the audio companions to this book—interview our children about what it was like to grow up with entrepreneur parents. Here's a slightly condensed version of what they said:

Q: What was it like when your parents worked at corporate jobs?

Alexander: My dad traveled a lot. He left very early in the morning, and the only way I'd ever see him is if I woke up very early too. If I did that, I could watch him head out the door, and then I'd have to go back to bed.

Genevieve: I remember being picked up late from school and not seeing them until nighttime. They were both pretty stressed out a lot of the time.

Q: What happened when your parents transitioned to owning their own business and working from home?

Alexander: It really improved my childhood a great deal. They had a lot more flexibility to spend time with me, and do things like take me places after school. They were also way less stressed out.

Genevieve: They were around a lot more. A lot of my friends never saw their parents because they got home so late from work, but my parents were always home. I had to keep explaining to my friends what they did for work, because no one understood it.

Q: *You both worked for the business for a while. What kinds of jobs did you do for your parents?*

Alexander: Genevieve and I originally stuffed envelopes, until they gave that job to somebody else. Then I catalogued which companies paid their bills on time and which did not. Once I got to college, I had too much schoolwork, so I had to stop.

Q: *What did you guys learn from working for the business?*

Alexander: I don't know if I particularly want to stuff envelopes ever again. But I learned to work carefully and quickly, and I think overall it was a good experience.

Genevieve: I learned I do not want a desk job. Ever. I cannot imagine sitting there doing the same thing over and over again for hours on end.

Q: *What was the downside of your parents being entrepreneurial?*

Alexander: They were always around.

Genevieve: They were always home. All the time.

Q: *What was it like watching your mom and dad working together?*

Alexander: It was interesting, because they worked very smoothly together. They didn't yell at each other that often. If things didn't go right, they resolved it peacefully instead of screaming. They also just saw each other more, and I think they've gotten closer because of that.

Genevieve: It was surprisingly calm, because I know that a lot of business partners do get into work-related arguments, and then their relationship suffers. It was interesting how they were able to avoid that and keep a good relationship outside of work.

Q: What have you guys learned about business?

Alexander: People don't pay their bills. And a lot of times when they do pay, it's not even the full amount. I remember reading lots of email excuses from people who wouldn't cough up the rest of the money they owed until my parents had called and emailed several times.

Genevieve: I learned that sometimes you have to take risks and that working hard through the ups and downs will eventually pay off. Every time you work through a problem you learn how to do it better and faster, so that the next time it happens you can deal with it more effectively.

Q: How do you think your lives have been different from the lives of your friends whose parents work in traditional jobs?

Alexander: I know a lot of my friends didn't get to spend a lot of time with their parents, because they were always working, especially their dads.

Q: Do you think you'll want to work for someone else when you grow up or have your own business like your parents?

Alexander: I want to be an engineer, so I know I will definitely work for someone else, at least at first. But I haven't decided yet whether or not I'd eventually like to own my own company.

Genevieve: All I really know is I definitely don't want to be working a desk job. Because of that, I might have to start off working for somebody, but in the future I might work for myself.

Q: What do you think of your parents writing this book?

Alexander: I'm interested to see how well it does.

Genevieve: I think it's cool that they'll be able to help more people than they do with just their speeches. They love to help people learn from their experiences and hopefully motivate others to become successful entrepreneurs, which is great.

So there you have it. Unsurprisingly, Alexander and Genevieve were not always thrilled to have us around the house all the time, but in the long run we were all able to enjoy a healthy, balanced family life. As we had hoped, our kids feel empowered to follow whatever path they choose, rather than pressured to follow in our footsteps. We are grateful that we were able to give them so many opportunities, and that we didn't have to miss the soccer tournaments and school assemblies to do so. The older they get, the more precious all those memories become.

INDEX

. . . .

Note, Page numbers followed by a *t* indicate a table.

CREDITS

. . . .

Publisher/Editorial Director: Michael Roney

Designer/Illustrator: Kendra Cagle

Proofreader: Maureen Moriarty

Indexer: Karl Ackley

Contact: info@highpointpubs.com

HIGHPOINT
E X E C U T I V E
PUBLISHING
Extend your strategic reach

wwww.highpointpubs.com

CPSIA information can be obtained
at www.ICGtesting.com
Printed in the USA
LVOW07*0550290917

550364LV00003B/3/P

9 780997 415797